IMAGES
of America

THE IRISH
IN HAVERHILL
MASSACHUSETTS
VOLUME II

WEDDING AT SAINT JAMES CHURCH. A. Elizabeth Fitzgerald married Arthur Walch about 1912. Arthur Walch appears in the City Directory for the first time in 1911, and he is listed as a clerk and as a boarder in a house on Portland Street, about one block away from where the Fitzgeralds lived. Two years later he is listed as living in his own home on Fifth Avenue with his wife, Elizabeth. Annie Elizabeth, born in 1884, was the daughter of Patrick J. and Annie (McNamara) Fitzgerald (at right in the picture). Raymond V. McNamara, the bride's cousin, is in the back row, second from the left. Her attendants are her two youngest sisters, Marion and Hazel. The gowns, the hats, the men's formal wear, and all the finery display the height of high fashion.

Cover: **IRISH STEP DANCERS, STUDENTS OF DANIEL LEAHY.** More than one hundred years after the first great influx of Irish immigrants to Haverhill, the traditional dances were still being taught. Daniel Leahy Jr. led his pupils through the intricacies of jigs, reels, and hornpipes throughout the 1960s and 1970s. This photo was taken in 1968. The dancers, from left to right, are: Andrea Peterson, Sheila Connor, Mary Daly, Barbara Donovan, Paula Phillips, and Jane Meader.

IMAGES
of America

THE IRISH
IN HAVERHILL
MASSACHUSETTS
VOLUME II

Dr. Patricia Trainor O'Malley

ARCADIA

Published by Arcadia Publishing,
an imprint of Tempus Publishing, Inc.
2 Cumberland Street
Charleston, SC 29401

Printed in Great Britain.

Library of Congress Catalog Card Number: 99-60293

For all general information contact Arcadia Publishing at:
Telephone 843-853-2070
Fax 843-853-0044
E-Mail arcadia@charleston.net

For customer service and orders:
Toll-Free 1-888-313-BOOK

Visit us on the internet at http://www.arcadiaimages.com

*To all who made the long voyage, whether by sailing ship from Galway,
steamship from Cobh, or Aer Lingus from Shannon.
They are yet alive in their photographs!*

DANIEL LEAHY SR., TRADITIONAL MUSICIAN. Dan Leahy had learned to play the fiddle in his home town of Mount Collins, Co. Limerick. He brought his talent with him to Haverhill in 1907 and raised his family to know and love Irish song and dance. He often played at Irish dances and kitchen "rackets," the informal parties that the immigrants loved.

CONTENTS

has ever been able to do. A photograph of a loved one keeps that person "alive" long after the obituaries have been written and the sods laid on the grave. We offer this collection of photographs to help teach, to remember, and to enjoy.

Acknowledgments

Daniel J. Leahy
Irene Fitzgerald
Rose Leeman Scamporino
Mark Cronin
Ann Dorsey Euele
Nancy Stolberg
Cathleen Cronin Regan
Helen Sullivan
Mary Horgan McDermott
Helen Horgan Ashton
Mary E. Gavin
Rachel McCarthy Mitchell
Richard Burchell
Edward Coakley
Ann Boland Messer
Margaret Cotter Ruth
Edward Wholley
Margaret Archambault Sullivan
Sue Dorsey Fici
Carol A. Bixby
Joan Hefferan McCarthy
John J. Ryan, III
Claire Emilio Wilson
Hilda Burns Kasianchuk
Virginia Sawyer Carbone
Martin Kelly
Kathie Tracy Scriber
Karen Harrigan Dewhurst
Arlene Tetrault
Dorothy Riley

Joan Healey Drapeau
Elaine Taffe
Michael Frank O'Dea
John and Mary Moynihan Caron
Edward Mahoney
Robert Gardella
Evelyn Malone Morin
Bernard J. Gallagher
Frances Donovan Cotton
Haverhill Historical Society
John Driscoll
Helen Carney Gobbi
Eileen Cronin Breglia
James Glispin
Esther Leary O'Shea
Alice McAleer Lyons
Paul Bresnahan
Patricia Ambrose Miller
Helen Ryan
Edith Perkins Guerin
Janice Carrigg Anderson
Ann McCarthy Lynn
Robert Roche
James Flaherty
Anna O'Brien O'Connor
James P. Cleary, III
Bridey Hourihan Hubley
Ann Linehan Drelick
Deputy Chief Donald Shea
Haverhill Public Library, Special Collections

One

THE NINETEENTH-
CENTURY IMMIGRANTS

JAMES AND MARY CRONIN AND CHILDREN. James Cronin was born in Co. Cork in 1858, and he immigrated to Boston in 1879. He was a morocco finisher in a tannery when he married Mary V. Cummings in 1884. She had been born in Wales of Irish parents and immigrated in 1875. This family picture appears to have been taken for their 25th wedding anniversary in 1909, by which time James had left the tannery and opened a grocery store on Kimball Street in the Acre. Pictured from left to right are: (front) Ellen (born 1888), James and Mary V. Cronin, Andrew (1893), and William (1901); (rear) Edward (1898), Mary (1895), James (1890), John (1886), Frank (1892), and Julia (1889).

CAPT. MICHAEL C. MCNAMARA. Michael McNamara was a recently married shoemaker when the Civil War broke out. He became a leader in organizing his fellow Irish immigrants in the Haverhill area into their own Company. The group was made a part of the 17th Regiment, and McNamara was elected its captain. A fellow Irish officer from Haverhill, Henry Splaine, eventually became colonel, commanding the entire regiment. McNamara is #4 in this photographic collage of officers of the 17th Regiment.

Rev. John T. McDonnell, O.P. Fr. McDonnell arrived in Haverhill in 1850 as a recently ordained 28 year old, with instructions to create a parish and build a church for the Catholics in the area, an area that extended to Exeter, New Hampshire. The overwhelming majority of those Catholics were very recent Irish immigrants. McDonnell oversaw the building of the first church, named for St. Gregory. The initials after his name indicate that he was a member of the Order of Preachers, more commonly known as Dominicans. Fr. McDonnell was transferred to Dover, New Hampshire, in 1872.

The "Miraculous Shrine" at St. Gregory's School. The original St. Gregory's Church was converted to a school when the larger St. James Church was built. The old building was destroyed by fire in 1901. When the ruins were searched, this classroom shrine to St. Joseph, with its lace canopy and the picture of St. Patrick, were discovered to be untouched by the flames, though all around it lay the charred ruins of the classroom in which it was located.

TIMOTHY DONOVAN, MERCHANT. Tim Donovan emigrated from Ballydehob, Co. Cork, in 1869, along with his parents, Michael Donovan and Julia Mahoney, a sister, Catherine, and brothers John, Jeremiah, Patrick, and Michael. Tim married Nelly Loftias in 1879 and they had eight children: Timothy, John, Michael, Julia, Thomas, Eleanor and Mary (both of whom died in infancy), and Raymond. Donovan operated both a grocery store and a paint store. In addition, he owned a significant amount of real estate in the Sargent Square area, now known as Lafayette Square. Tim died in 1924.

ELLEN "NELLY" LOFTIAS. Nelly was born in Co. Galway in 1848 and immigrated to Canada as a young girl. Family tradition is that her mother placed her and her sister on board a ship leaving Galway City without their prior knowledge. An Amesbury doctor met the two young girls in Canada and brought them to the United States in 1869. Nelly met and married Tim Donovan in 1879. Her son Tim took over the family businesses, and Michael worked with him. Son John became a doctor and Raymond a pharmacist. Tom, a painter, died from the effects of his WW I service. Daughter Julia married Edward Fitzgerald (see p. 38). Nelly died in 1915.

TIM DONOVAN'S GROCERY STORE. This store was located at 75 Lafayette Square, then known as Sargent's Square. The building was on the west side of the square, approximately where Marble Motors is located. Tim began the business about 1885. The store offered "Groceries and Provisions" as well as "West Indies Goods," meaning coffee, sugar, and spices. Shown from left to right are: Tim Jr. (born 1883), Tom (born 1888), and Tim Sr. The Donovan family lived above the store. This photo was taken in 1895.

PATRICK J. AND ANNIE FITZGERALD. "P J " Fitzgerald emigrated from Tralee, Co. Kerry, with his parents, John and Mary (Harrington), and brothers Michael, John, David, and James. Though the parents were illiterate, their children were educated. Patrick had been trained by the Christian Brothers to a level equivalent of a high school education. By 1880 he and his brothers John and James had their own heel manufacturing business in Haverhill. Brother Michael moved out to Kenoza Street in the city's East Parish, where he established the family farm, which is still in operation. Brother David was a stone mason. Patrick married West Newbury native Annie McNamara in 1881. The McNamaras were prominent in Democratic politics as well as in the shoe industry in Haverhill.

IRISH DOMESTICS AND FRIENDS. Irish immigration came in waves to Haverhill. There was very little before the 1850s, yet, by 1860, there were over a thousand native Irish living in Greater Haverhill. Immigration slowed down markedly during the 1860s and 1870s because of the American Civil War and improvements in Ireland. New ideas about land inheritance and inexpensive steamship rates led to a second wave of immigration in the 1880s, which continued until WW I. Seated right in this mid-1890s photograph is Ellen McCarthy, and standing is her brother Tim and childhood friend, Nelly Conley, all of whom came from Leap, Co. Cork. Ellen and Nelly worked for years as cooks and maids.

JOHANNA MCCARTHY FITZGERALD. Johanna McCarthy was born in Rathmore, Co. Kerry, in 1863. She immigrated to Haverhill in 1881 and worked as a domestic at Bradford Academy. She married John Dennis Fitzgerald in 1887. He came from the Rathmore area also and had immigrated in 1883. They bought a house at 75 Fifth Avenue in 1896, when they had four children (see p. 76). John worked as a teamster, and one of their sons, Daniel, no relation to P.J. Fitzgerald, served as chairman of the Haverhill Board of Assessors.

BARTHOLOMEW AND MARY MORIARTY AND HELEN. "Bat" Moriarty was born in Tralee, Co. Kerry, in 1866. He immigrated with his parents in 1882 to Springfield, Massachusetts, where he was trained as a tailor. He married Mary Twomey, born in Lawrence of Irish parents, in 1893. She listed her occupation on the marriage license as tailoress. The Moriartys moved to Haverhill where two daughters were born. Bat Moriarty was in the tailoring business for over 40 years, mostly at 21 Emerson Street. The family home was at 24 Lexington Avenue, Bradford. Daughter Helen became a school teacher, and daughter Catherine married John Cronin (see p. 9). Mary Moriarty died in 1920, and Bat died three years later.

ANNIE DACEY FLAVIN STANTON. Annie was born in Roscarberry, Co. Cork, in 1868. She came to Haverhill in 1889, one of five in her family to do so. She worked as a domestic until her marriage to Michael Flavin in 1895. She was soon left a widow and her only child died, so in 1900 she was once again working as a servant in a private house. Later, she married a widower, John Stanton. Stanton was a shoeworker who lived at 2 Lovejoy Street, Bradford.

JOHANNAH HORGAN.
"Hannah" Horgan was born in Banteer, Co. Cork, in 1863. She immigrated in 1882 and lived with an aunt in West Newbury until she married Patrick Dacey in 1891. This was the first of three marriages of Daceys to Horgans. The family motto was "You can't throw a stone at a Dacey without hitting a Horgan!" Pat was the brother of Annie Dacey and the first in the family to come to Haverhill. He immigrated in 1888 and worked as a stone mason. Hannah gave birth to ten children, six of whom survived to adulthood: Agnes, John, Madeline, Irene, Marion, and Patrick Sarsfield. Patrick died in 1917 when his youngest children were still in school. It was that same year that this picture of Hannah with her oldest son, Jack, was taken.

HANNAH HORGAN DACEY. Hannah Dacey was left a widow in 1917, but she was surrounded not only by her children but by numerous relatives on both sides of the family. Patrick Dacey's brother John immigrated in 1891 and four years later married Mary Horgan. The Dacey brothers bought a two-family house on Dexter Street, which provided room not only for the Dacey children, but also for other members of the family as they arrived from Ireland. For example, in 1900, Patrick, Daniel, and Bartholomew Horgan were all living with their sisters and brothers-in-law. Hannah Dacey died in 1934, the year this photo was taken. Hannah, seated, is shown with her son Patrick Sarsfield, left, and a cousin, Denis Donoghue. Sarsfield carries the name of a famous 18th-century Irish patriot.

CORNELIUS AND ELLEN DACEY HORGAN. Con and Ellen were the third marriage between Daceys and Horgans. Con and Nelly were born in 1874, and both immigrated at 16 years old in 1890. They were married in 1901. Con worked in a shoe factory. Pictured from left to right are: (front) Alice, Julia, and Mary Horgan; (middle) Bob Horgan, Ellen Dacey Horgan, and Jack Lane; (rear) Bill Lane and "Con" Horgan. One other Dacey in Haverhill was Margaret. She married James Farley, a Co. Longford native. There is a stone in St. James Cemetery marked "In memory of our beloved mother, Nora Dacey, 1837–1912." Nora Dillon Dacey was the mother of the Daceys.

BARTHOLOMEW AND MARGARET KELLEHER HORGAN WITH SON GERALD. "Bat" Horgan was born in 1879 and immigrated in 1897. In 1907, he married Margaret Kelleher, who had immigrated in 1896. The Horgans had nine children. This photo was taken before son Gerald was ordained to the priesthood in 1947, but because his mother was very ill, he posed with his Roman collar on. Other Horgans in Haverhill were Patrick, who married Mary O'Connor and had 11 children (see p. 81); Daniel, who wed Catherine Flavin and had nine children; John, who wed Julia Kelleher, sister of Margaret, parents of eight children; Julia, who wed Henry Murphy and had two children; and Timothy, the first to immigrate. He married Nora O'Leary in 1885, had seven children, and returned to Ireland to take over the family farm.

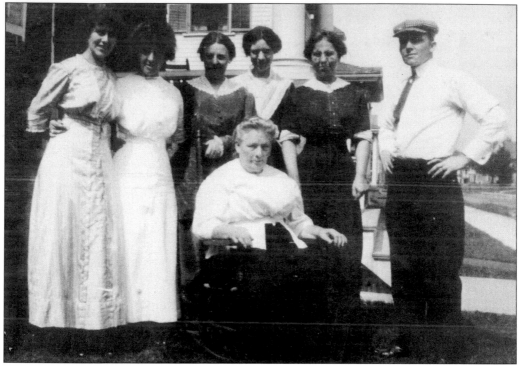

BRIDGET FOLEY GAVIN. Bridget, born in 1853, immigrated in 1868. After her husband, Dennis, died in 1900, Bridget was employed as a nurse. By 1910, the family had moved to the newly developed Chandler Street in Bradford. Bridget, seated, is shown with some of her children. From left to right are: Esther, Mary (Mame), two unidentified women, Martha (Mattie), and Joseph. Bridget died in 1926.

DENNIS GAVIN. Dennis was an immigrant from County Clare. He worked as a laborer and lived with his wife, Bridget Foley, at 30 Lewis Street. They had nine children, eight of whom were alive in 1900. They included: Andrew, 24; Mary, 23; Ellen, 19; Martha, 18; Alice, 15; William, 12; Joseph, ten; and Esther, eight. Dennis died of pneumonia in March 1900 at the age of 55. Alice, Joseph, and Esther were still in school. All of the older children were employed as shoe workers. Dennis's son Bill, who was 12 when Dennis died, would join the police force and rise to the rank of deputy chief.

MARY O'LEARY McCARTHY.
"Minnie" O'Leary was born in
Rathmore, Co. Kerry, in 1868.
Rathmore was home for a great
number of Haverhill Irish
immigrants. Minnie immigrated in
1881. It is family tradition that
Minnie was so lovely, that "the
dance stopped when she walked
into the room." In September 1894
she married American-born Dennis
McCarthy. They made their home
in the old Ward 5, first on Beach
Street, and later at 446 Washington
Street. The McCarthys had five
sons: Warren, Lawrence, John,
George, and Arthur, and two
daughters: Alice and Mary. Both
daughters died in childhood.
Minnie died in 1943.

DENNIS L. McCARTHY. Dennis,
Minnie's husband, was born in
Lawrence in 1864. He moved to
Haverhill at his marriage. For many
years he ran a large liquor retail
business on River Street under the
name of D.L. McCarthy & Co. After
retiring from that business in 1914,
Dennis worked for the Arlington
Mills in Lawrence for 15 years. He
died of a heart attack at the age of 67
in 1934.

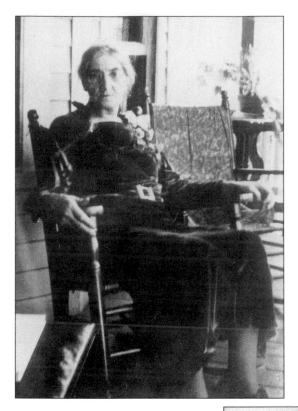

NORA HAYES SULLIVAN. Nora had been born in Killarney, Co. Kerry, in 1869. She immigrated in 1885 and worked as a housekeeper until her marriage to American-born Daniel Sullivan in 1895. In 1900 the Sullivans were living on Front Street, Bradford, with their four daughters and Nora's nephew. She was earning extra money as a presser of hats at the nearby Hat Factory on Railroad Avenue. By 1920, there were seven children, and all were living at the family home on High Street (now Germain Avenue), Bradford. Nora died in 1949.

DANIEL SULLIVAN. Dan was born in Haverhill in 1873, the son of Daniel Sullivan and Mary Santry, who had emigrated from Co. Cork. Young Dan was employed as a brick layer. He had seven brothers and sisters. Two of his nephews, Daniel Sullivan and Daniel Cooper, were killed in WW I (see p.83). In later years, Dan was employed as a hatter. By the mid-1920s, the Sullivans were living on Leonard Avenue, Bradford, which was just being developed. Dan died in 1958.

MARGARET O'CONNELL DEVLIN AND GRANDSON. Margaret was born in Ireland in 1842 and immigrated to America in 1863. She married John Devlin in 1873. Born in Ireland in 1844, he immigrated in 1872 and was a laborer. The Devlins lived at 69 Primrose Street near 8th Avenue and had four children. John had died by 1910, and Margaret moved around the corner to her daughter, Martha Devlin Dorsey's, house on 8th Avenue. She is shown here with her grandson, Luke Dorsey, son of Martha and Michael Dorsey Jr. Margaret died in 1924.

MR. AND MRS. PATRICK NOONAN. Margaret Rice married Patrick Noonan in 1895. Patrick had been born in Ballyporeen, Co. Tipperary, in 1871 and immigrated in 1888. He was a brother to Michael Donahue Noonan (see p. 87). Margaret, born in 1869, had immigrated in 1889. For many years, the Noonans lived on Oak Terrace while Patrick worked as a dyer in the Stevens Mills. They later moved to Chandler Street, Bradford. They had three children: Thomas, who was a funeral director, Mary, a school teacher at the Cogswell and Peabody Schools, and Margaret, a nurse, who took over her brother's business. The Noonans are shown above on vacation in No. Conway, New Hampshire, in 1925. Margaret died in 1928 and Patrick in 1933.

MICHAEL COAKLEY AND SISTER NORA. The Coakleys had emigrated from Castle Gregory, Co. Kerry. Michael, the oldest, was born in 1867 and immigrated in 1888. He married Nora Kelley in 1895 and they had four children. After Nora died, he remarried and had two more children, including Edward, a well-known Haverhill culinary artist. Michael worked as a laborer for the city for years. His home was at 27 Middlesex Street, Bradford. He and his sister, Nora Coakley O'Connor of Lawrence, made headline news in 1930 when it was reported that a brother in Australia had died leaving a fortune in gold nuggets. The actual inheritance was small but it made for some excitement for a while.

MAURICE FITZGERALD AND "THE LADY." Maurice Fitzgerald, born in 1865, emigrated from Co. Limerick in 1882. He worked for a while as a teamster for a lumber company then purchased a saloon in Sargent's (Lafayette) Square near the Stevens Woolen Mills. His offer of a free lunch with every pint of beer made his business prosper. Later, he went into real estate, erecting many of the houses on Lockwood Street in Bradford. He married Julia Mahoney in 1895. She emigrated from Rock Chapel, Co. Cork, in 1889. A door-to-door salesman's query about "the lady of the house" led to Maurice referring to his wife from that time on as "the Lady." They are shown here at the wedding of her niece Mary Linnehan to William P. Boland in 1925. Pictured from left to right are: Julia Linnehan, Maurice Fitzgerald, Julia Mahoney Fitzgerald, Mary Mahoney Linnehan, and Mary Linnehan Boland.

JOHN F. COTTER. John Cotter, a shoe cutter, served as a Haverhill City Councillor in 1896 and 1897. He had been born in Ballydehob, Co. Cork, in 1860 and arrived in Boston in 1877. The witnesses at his naturalization were Con Driscoll (see p. 30) and Bernard Donahue (see p. 42). Jack married Mary Alice Sullivan in 1896 and by 1900 they had four children, one of whom, Richard, was burned to death as a child. Their home was at 67 Primrose Street, next door to John and Margaret Devlin. Later they moved to 233 Franklin Street. Jack died in 1934.

MARY ALICE SULLIVAN COTTER. Mary Alice was born in Goleen, Co. Cork, just south of Ballydehob, in 1874. She was the oldest of ten children. Eight came to Haverhill, but four of them returned to Goleen. "Minnie" immigrated in 1892 and married John Cotter four years later. By 1910, they had six living children: Katherine, Francis, Mary, John, Eileen, and Daniel. Minnie died a month after her husband in February 1934.

MARGARET CALLAHAN AND MICHAEL MELODY. Margaret Frances Callahan was born in Co. Cork in 1876 and immigrated with her sister Bess in 1888. Three years later their mother Catherine joined them. Margaret worked as a corder in a shoe factory until she married Michael Melody in 1895. Melody had emigrated from England in 1884. He was of Irish descent. The Melodys first lived on Sheridan Street but moved to 37 Charles Street into a 1790s-era house that faced St. James High School. They had seven children: Sabena Esther, Eugene Walter, Mary K., John, Marguerite, Helen, and Elizabeth. Michael died in 1924 and Margaret in 1942.

MICHAEL AND MARY WHOOLEY. Civil authorities could not agree on how to spell Michael's name. On his wedding certificate, he is "Hooley." In the 1900 City Directory, he is "Wholey." And in the Census of the same year, he is "Whorley." The family's choice was "Whooley." Michael and Mary came from the area of Skibbereen, Co. Cork. Michael immigrated in 1882 and worked as a teamster. Mary Murphy immigrated in 1885 and did housework before marrying Michael in 1891. By 1910, Mary had borne seven children: John, Michael, Katherine, Leo, Mary, William, and Edward. Michael drove a team for a coal company.

MICHAEL DORSEY SR. AND SON THOMAS.
Michael Dorsey emigrated from Co. Clare in 1857 and, soon after he arrived, married Annie Norton, who had immigrated in 1848. In 1870, which is about when this tintype appears to have been taken, the Dorseys were living on Maple Street. Michael, 44, worked in a shoe factory. Annie, 37, had five children under the age of ten: Mary J., Annie, Kate, Thomas, and Luke. Two additional children, Ellen and Michael Jr., would be born in the 1870s. Eventually Michael bought a home at 125 8th Avenue, which still remains in the family.

THE HAUGHEY FAMILY. Bernard Haughey was born in Co. Armagh in the midst of the Great Famine, and came to America in 1850. His family settled in Dover, New Hampshire. His wife Sarah was born in Dover in 1858 of parents from Co. Armagh. Bernard and Sarah were married in Dover in 1878, and their first two children, Edward and Catherine, were born there. It may have been at the suggestion of Fr. John McDonnell, pastor of the Catholic Church in Dover (see p. 11), that the family decided to move to Haverhill in 1885. Bernard, a shoe cutter, his family, and his sister Mary, a hat maker, lived in the Hilldale Avenue area. Bernard died in 1910 after the family moved to Cambridge. Pictured from left to right are: (front) Helen "Loretta" Haughey (1885–1947), Edward (1879–1939), Bernard (1847–1910), and Sarah (1858–1936).

JOHN AND CATHERINE MURPHY HEFFERAN. John Hefferan was born in Drumline, Co. Fermanagh, in 1865. He immigrated to So. Groveland in 1880 and went to work in the woolen mill in that town. He married Catherine Murphy in 1888. She had been born in Ayers Village, Haverhill, in 1863. According to the 1900 Census, "Johnny" Hefferan had become a farmer and Catherine had given birth to the first five of their seven children. Also in the household was John's 21-year-old brother, Joseph, and Catherine's widowed father, Thomas Murphy. Murphy was 66, had immigrated in 1851, and was now a farm laborer, presumably for his son-in-law John. The Hefferans celebrated their 50th wedding anniversary in 1938.

REV. JAMES O'DOUGHERTY, WORLD TRAVELER. Fr. O'Dougherty, born in Co. Donegal in 1848, became the fourth pastor of St. Gregory's Parish in 1878. Within three years he had begun construction on a new church at the corner of Primrose and Winter Streets. The parish was re-named in honor St. James, Fr. O'Dougherty's patron saint. He turned the old St. Gregory's Church into a grammar school, built a high school and parish hall, and when the grammar school burned, replaced it with a new brick structure. In his later years, he took to travelling. Here, a very stout Fr. O'Dougherty bestrides a camel in Egypt. What the Sphinx thought of this sight, he did not say.

Two

THE IMMIGRANTS'
CHILDREN

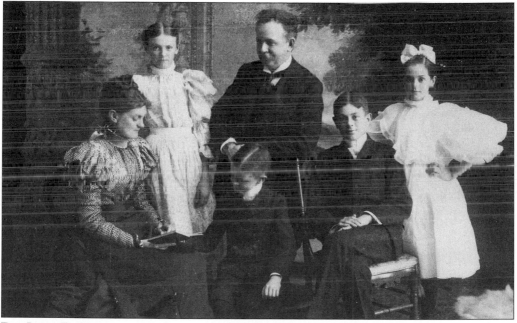

DR. JOHN F. CROSTON AND FAMILY. Haverhill's beloved Dr. John Croston (1855–1921) was born in Bradford of Co. Cork parents. He earned his medical degree from New York University and set up practice in Haverhill in 1880. Pictured from left to right are: (seated) Dr. John's wife, Mary Frances Farrell (1858–1909), and sons George (1886–1960) and Francis (1882–1952); (rear) George's twin sister R. Elaine (1886–1961), Dr. John, and Mary (1884–1970). None of the Croston children married. Elaine and Mary were longtime teachers in the Haverhill schools. The annual prize for poetry at the Haverhill High School commencement is named in memory of R. Elaine Croston.

REV. JOHN GRAHAM. Fr. Graham was the first pastor of Sacred Hearts Church, Bradford. He was born in Boston in 1863 and raised in Haverhill. His father, Hugh, emigrated from Co. Armagh in 1849. Hugh died of Chronic Bright's Disease in 1882, at the age of 50, and his wife, Mary Sullivan, died of phthisis in 1888. From 1889 until becoming pastor in Bradford, Fr. Graham was a curate at St. James Parish. He returned there to become its pastor in 1913, succeeding Fr. O'Dougherty. Fr. Graham is remembered as the pastor who initiated the sports program at St. James High School, built the Athletic Park, and greatly expanded St. James Cemetery. But more than those physical actions, he is remembered for his kindnesses and deep spirituality.

JOHN BURNS. Burns was born in New York in 1865 of Irish parents. His wife, Frances J. O'Brien, who he married in 1894, had been born in 1870 in Massachusetts of Irish parents. John was a shoe cutter and, later, a foreman in local shoe shops. He served as Chief Ranger of the Foresters, and was a leading figure in the Hibernians and the Fr. Matthew Total Abstinence Society. The Burns family lived on Primrose Street, and later moved to So. Williams Street in Bradford. They had a son, Joseph Alva (see p. 90), and a daughter Hilda.

MARY REARDON. Mary was born in Haverhill in 1869 to Dennis Reardon, a shoemaker born in Ireland, and Ellen Lynch Brown, a widow, also from Ireland. Dennis took his own life in 1884 and a few years later, in 1893, Ellen died of exposure and general debility. Mary was taken into the home of Patrick and Catherine Thynne. She eventually married John Gindorff of Chicago, where this picture was taken.

JAMES, ANNIE, AND JOHN KELLY. The Kellys were the children of Martin Kelly from Galway and Elizabeth (Lizzie) Gavin from Roscommon. John, right, the eldest of four surviving children, was born about 1876. He became a shoe cutter and died in 1920. James, on the left, was a member of the police department for 21 years. He died in 1934. Annie, center, was born in 1881, graduated from Haverhill High School in 1900, and from McIntosh Business School. She was a legal secretary, and secretary for the License Commission. Later she became associated with her younger brother, Frank (see p. 41), in the auto business. They held the Hudson-Essex franchise in Haverhill. Annie died in 1949.

THOMAS F. WALDRON AND CO-WORKERS. Thomas Waldron, center, owned a sole manufacturing business in the basement of 74 Washington Street. He was the son of Michael Waldron (1825–1903) and Bridget Hanley (1825–1898). They were Irish immigrants who were married in Haverhill in 1853. Thomas was born in 1857. The 1870 Federal Census listed Michael as the owner of a shoe factory, with real estate worth $2,500. In 1900, Thomas and his wife, Mary A. Connor, and their son Clement were living at 8 Lawrence Street. By 1910, he had moved to 55 Kenoza Avenue. His moulded counters business was then located on Wingate Street. Thomas died in 1951, and his wife two years earlier.

FOUR YOUNG "SPORTS." These four young men shared a love for baseball and all played on an 1887 Bradford team. A photo of that team, with all players named, still exists (see Volume I). Pictured from left to right are, Thomas Dorsey (see p. 34), Bill McDonald, and Johnny Connor, who were all born in Haverhill of Irish parents. Standing at right is Cornelius Patrick "Connie" Driscoll, born in Drishane, Co. Cork, in 1864. Driscoll played, managed, or owned baseball teams for most of the rest of his life.

SAINT JAMES CHURCH ALTAR BOYS, C. 1896. Pictured from left to right are: (front row) Augustine "Gus" Hurley, born 1888 to immigrants Tim and Honoria; future bishop Daniel Desmond, born 1884 to immigrants Daniel and Catherine; Lawrence McNamara, born 1888 to shoe man S Burton and Joanna, Massachusetts natives; John E. McDonald, born 1887 to Thomas, a wine merchant, and Margrett, both born locally; (second row) George Hurley, born 1886, brother to Gus; Cornelius Sullivan, born in New Hampshire in 1884 to immigrants Timothy and Johanna; future judge Daniel Cavan, born 1885 to immigrants Jeremiah and Mary (Sullivan); Richard Fitzgerald, born 1886 to P.J. and Annie (McNamara) (see p. 38); (third row) future doctor Lawrence Kelley, born 1887 to locally born Thomas, who ran a periodicals store, and Catherine; Frank Tuck, born 1887 to Francis, of English descent, and Mary (Smith), born in Canada of Irish parents; Richard Barry, born in 1886 to Edward, a hatter, and Bridget, an immigrant; Raymond Murphy, born 1888, the son of John and Johanna, both locally born; Philip Sullivan of 29 John St., born in 1888 to immigrants Mary and Philip, a grocer (the father died in 1889); T. Joseph McAuliffe, 31 North St., born 1887 to Catherine and Thomas (Thomas was a superintendent who died about 1898); (fourth row) Joseph Barrett, born 1885 to immigrants John and Margaret (Sullivan); John McNamara, born 1880 to shoe man Lott and Elizabeth (Downer); Jerome Burke, born 1884 to immigrants Daniel and Catherine; Joseph Ryan, born 1883 to immigrants Patrick and Ellen (Shaw); Arthur Mullen, 221 Winter St., born 1884, to Annie and Alexander, a shoemaker who was dead by 1891; Edward "Bodger" Carroll, son of Roger, a barber, and Mary. Carroll was the famed coach for the championship sports teams at St. James High School in the 1920s. The teams were managed by his fellow altar boy, Gus Hurley.

ALBION TRACY, SCOTS-IRISH. Albion and his wife Addie do not fit the chapter's title of "The Immigrants' Children." They came from that earlier line of inheritance, the Scots-Irish immigration of the 18th century. Albion was born in Maine in 1860 of native-Maine parents. He married Addie Doherty in 1881, and in 1900 they were living at 31 Whittier Street in the old Ward 4. Albion was a shoemaker, and all six of his children were alive and living at home when the 1900 Census was taken. He died in 1938.

ADDIE DOHERTY TRACY. Addie was born in Gorham, Maine, in 1861 and, like her husband Albion, was of Scots-Irish descent. In 1917, Addie and her husband were living at 12 Greenleaf Street in Bradford. Two of their sons, George and Clarence, were serving in the Army. While riding in an electric car, Addie took fright at a flashing light, thinking it was lightning, and jumped from the car, fracturing her skull. She lingered in the hospital long enough for her sons to be allowed brief furloughs to see her. She died the day after they arrived home.

JOHN FRANCIS AND ROSANA BOULANGER MCCORMICK. John McCormick was the grandson of immigrants Patrick McCormick and Annie Cline. Annie's brother Patrick married McCormick's sister Mary, and they were the parents of the celebrated Maggie Cline (see p.6). John's father, Thomas McCormick, married Katie McLaughlin. She was the daughter of the stone carver Patrick McLaughlin, who made the Civil War Memorial statue in Monument Square. McCormicks, Clines, and McLaughlins were among Haverhill's pioneering Irish families. John was a shoe cutter, born in 1879. He married Rosana Boulanger, of French-Canadian ancestry, in 1900. They had ten children and eventually moved to Georgetown where they had a small country store. Rosana died in 1931 and John in 1961.

PATRICK AND MARGARET HARRIGAN. Patrick Harrigan was the son of Dennis, a day laborer who immigrated in 1863, and Mary Mahoney, who immigrated in 1870. Dennis and Mary were married in 1874, and Patrick was born a year later. Pat was employed as a shoe cutter until 1930 when he became the janitor for city hall on Main Street. He is shown here with his wife Margaret (Surrette) and children: Mary, John Rolland, Leo, and Thomas. Leo had been born in 1903, so this picture was taken about 1906.

HUNTING CAMP, MOOSEHEAD LAKE, MAINE. One sign of the growing prosperity of the Irish-American community in Haverhill was the increasing popularity of vacations. Beach houses proliferated at Salisbury and Hampton Beaches, and "a week at the beach" became an annual event. Yet others followed the "strenuous life," advocated by President Teddy Roosevelt, and took off into the wilderness on hunting and fishing trips. Here, three Dorsey brothers pose on the porch of a hunting lodge in Moosehead Lake, Maine, probably in the first years of the 20th century. From left to right are, Tom, Mike Jr., and Luke. Tom, the eldest of the brothers, was born in 1867, Luke in 1870, and Mike Jr. in 1874. They were the sons of Michael and Ann (Norton). The woman on the left is thought to have been the caretaker of the camp.

LUKE DORSEY, BALLPLAYER. Baseball was a passion for young men in the late 19th and early 20th century, and the Dorsey brothers were no exception. All played on local semi-pro teams, as did their sister Ellen's husband, James "Scagey" Ryan. Luke made it into the New England-New York League. He is shown here in his Norwich, Connecticut team shirt. His career was cut short when he contracted consumption. He died in 1906 at the age of 36.

THE DORSEYS AT SALISBURY BEACH. Tom Dorsey had a family photo taken each year, usually during the family vacation. Whatever relatives were visiting at the time joined in the group. This is the 1912 picture. Pictured from left to right are, (front) Joe and Jim Dorsey; (second row) Jack Dorsey, cousin Mary Ryan (Ellen Dorsey's daughter), and Mary Dorsey; (back row) Alice Dorsey, Helen Ryan, Martha Devlin Dorsey (Michael's wife), Anna, Michael, Katie Dorsey (sister to Mike and Tom), Luke, Mary Maynard Dorsey (Tom's wife), and Tom Dorsey.

DORSEYS, RYANS, AND ROCHES AT SALISBURY BEACH, 1907. Pictured from left to right are, (front) Mary Ryan, Jim, Luke, Alice, and Joe Dorsey; (second row) Anna Dorsey and Katherine Roche; (third row) James "Scagey" Ryan (standing), Mary Maynard Dorsey (holding baby Mary Dorsey), unidentified woman, Bernadette Roche, and David Roche (standing right); (back row) Tom Dorsey, Ellen Dorsey Ryan, and Mary Dorsey Roche.

JAMES F. "WEEPING JIM" CAREY. James Carey was born in Haverhill in 1867 to immigrant parents James and Mary (Moriarty). He had been a shoe worker and a leader of the Great Shoe Strike of 1894. In the 1890s he entered politics and achieved national recognition. He was elected to the Haverhill City Council in 1897 as a Socialist, the first municipal official in the nation from that party. From 1899 to 1903 he was a Representative to the General Court in Boston, again as a Socialist. At the same time, John C. Chase was elected mayor of Haverhill, the first Socialist mayor in the United States. In later years, Carey was a Socialist Party organizer and a frequent, unsuccessful candidate for governor. His nickname came from his emotional cries for local reform.

SAINT JAMES HIGH SCHOOL, CLASS OF 1903. Identified are the following: Edward J. Fitzgerald, son of PJ and Annie (front left), and M. Pauline Newell (front, second from left). Also identified is Julia A. Donovan, daughter of Tim and Nellie (rear right). Edward and Julia were high school sweethearts who were married about 1912. Others in the class were: William Sherry (probably front center), Michael Hurley (probably front right), Jane McCrealey, Julia A. Powers, and Margaret M. Ring.

**MEDORA GORMAN FEEHAN,
PHARMACIST, BUSINESSWOMAN, WRITER.**
Medora Gorman was an extraordinary
woman. She was born in New York in
1877. Her grandfather had emigrated from
County Limerick. Her father, James,
moved his family to Haverhill where he
operated a shoe factory in Washington
Square. Medora graduated from Haverhill
High School in 1893, and, as a biographer
reported, she "early manifested a strong
character and intellectuality." Medora
completed the Massachusetts College of
Pharmacy in 1898 and was the first female
pharmacist in Haverhill. When her father
became ill, she took over his business and
successfully ran it until her marriage to
Charles Feehan in 1919. For the remainder
of her life until her death in 1952, she was
active in leading many women's
organizations. She was a well-known writer
of political and religious essays, and once
took public issue with Eleanor Roosevelt
over the question of divorce.

THE GORMAN CHILDREN. Soon after Medora Gorman's father moved to Haverhill, her
mother, Mary Conway, died. James Gorman then married Nellie Sargent, and they had nine
children, half-brothers and -sisters to Medora and her brother John. One son, James Henry Jr.,
died as an infant in 1891. The surviving children with their birth dates are from left to right:
(front) Esther (1888), Arthur (1892), Henry (1883), Alfred (1894), Frances (1885), and James
Howard (1896); (rear) William (1886) and Frank (1887).

THE FITZGERALD MEN. Patrick J. Fitzgerald, center, is with his four sons: Richard, born 1886 (see p. 31), Edward (1885–1946), "PJ," Gerald (1888–1920), and Frank, born 1892. PJ was a sole manufacturer, and though an immigrant, he was appointed a city assessor, a position he held for over 20 years. The Fitzgeralds are shown on the front lawn of their home at 44 Nichols Street at the corner of Fourth Avenue. The neighborhood has changed tremendously since this photograph was taken in the early 1900s. In 1910, all four sons are listed as working for their father in his heel manufacturer. Richard had married Eva Bolduc in 1909 and was living in Bradford. Edward and Gerald would marry soon after this. Frank continued to live at home and never married.

THE FITZGERALD WOMEN. Annie McNamara Fitzgerald is shown with her daughters and daughter-in-law. They are from left to right, (front) Marion (born 1896), who married James Ryan of Lawrence, and Hazel (born 1901), who married Charles Stevens; (back) Lillian (born 1889), who married Martin Collins; Helena Roche (1892–1953), who married Annie's son Gerald; Annie, who died in 1914; A. Elizabeth (born 1884), who married Arthur Walch (see p. 2); and Helen, born in 1891, who died of peritonitis in 1916. Two other daughters, Nellie (1882–3) and Mary Irene (1894–5), died in infancy.

THE HAUGHEY CHILDREN.
Catherine, standing, and
William Bernard Haughey,
left, were two of the four
children of Bernard and Sarah
Haughey (see p. 25). The
Haugheys moved to Haverhill
about 1885. William Bernard
was born ten years later in
1895. The Haugheys lived in
the Hilldale Avenue area
during most of their time in
Haverhill. Catherine
remembered having friends in
the neighborhood who spoke
French, and she still had the
memory of some French
expressions when she was an
elderly woman. She married
Charles Johnson in 1923.
William Bernard was born in
Haverhill and lived there for
the first ten years of his life.
He went on to graduate
from Boston College and
serve in WW I.

ST. JAMES HIGH CLASS OF 1911. Pictured from left to right are the following: (front) Florence
Moran, Douglas Porrell, Beatrice Bourque, John Linnehan, Anna Dorsey, Daniel Creed, and
Agnes Moynihan; (second row) unidentified, unidentified, Hannah O'Connell, Harriet
Wright, Kathleen Ring, Olive Keefe, Eva Dupre, and three unidentified; (back row) Mary
Costello, Veronica Cummings, Joseph Callahan, Raymond Donovan, Michael Keville, Albert
Quimby, Edward McKenna, J. Agnes Donovan, and Rebecca Carey. Others in the class were:
Antoinette Dugas, Agnes Fennelly, Irene Laganiere, Ruth Pothier, and Eva Phaneuf.

FR. MATTHEW TOTAL ABSTINENCE SOCIETY. The Fr. Matthew Society began its Haverhill chapter in 1889. John E. Maguire, a local shoe manufacturer, was the founder. The organization was named for the Irish priest who popularized the concept of a mutual support society for those men who would "take the pledge" to abstain from alcohol. The image of the Irishman with a fondness for "a wee drop" was rooted in reality. Another reality was that many of the first successful Irish in Haverhill had become so through the sales of liquor. But the rapid growth, and long-term success of the Fr. Matthew Society suggests another side to this image. This photo, based on the style of clothing, dates from very early in the organization's existence. Each year the Society would stage a parade in October. Each member wore the Society's "uniform" of a bowler hat and black suit, and carried a black thorn stick, or shillelagh. The man on the horse appears to be John E. Maguire. The first man standing, left, is Haber McKenna, an early leader of the group.

Three

IRISH *NEED* APPLY!

FRANK KELLY AND HIGH SCHOOL LATIN CLUB. There is a long standing tradition that 19th-century Irish immigrants were shut out of jobs because of discrimination. "No Irish Need Apply" is supposed to have been a ubiquitous sign. Yet there were those who broke through the barriers. Two areas that opened their doors were public education and the police force. Immigrants, and the children of immigrants, appear among the graduates of Haverhill High School and in the ranks of teachers as early as the 1870s. In like manner, immigrants and their children were able to join the police as early as the 1860s. This chapter is about those school graduates and those policemen. Pictured above is the Haverhill High School Latin Club in the early 1900s. Seated left is Frank Kelly, son of Martin and Elizabeth Kelly, and brother of John, James, and Annie (see p. 29).

DANIEL FLYNN, CLASS OF 1877. Dan Flynn was the son of James Flynn, a blacksmith who lived on Locust Street. James died in 1882 of heart disease. Dan's mother was Margaret Ellen, who died a widow, in 1891. Dan went to work for M.H. McCarthy, liquor dealer, where he was a clerk. His home was at 201 Winter Street. He married Sarah Elizabeth Finney from Summer Street. Sarah died in 1909. They had a son James (1888–1951) and a daughter Bertha, who taught school in Bradford for many years, and died in 1996 at the age of 102.

KATE TERESA CARROLL, CLASS OF 1878. Kate was the daughter of Thomas Carroll, who immigrated in 1849, and Margaret Power, who immigrated in 1847. Margaret Carroll died of pneumonia, in 1900 at the age of 60. Kate taught at the Primrose Street School and the Winter Street School. She later married Bernard Donahue, brother of Dr. Hugh Donahue. They had three sons, all of whom carried family names: Hugh, Bernard (see p. 124), and John. Bernard died in 1921, and Kate died 11 years later in 1932. She was 71 years old.

ANNIE PATRICIA ROCHE, CLASS OF 1883. Annie was the daughter of John Martin Roche, a Kerry immigrant and Haverhill's first Irish-born city councillor. John had been a grocer and emigration agent but moved to Hilldale Avenue to be a "gentleman farmer." He was struck and killed by a train in 1884 while crossing from one of his fields to another. Annie's mother was Brigid Shea. Annie was one of four sisters to enter teaching. For many years she was principal of the Wingate School. None of the sisters married. Annie died in 1950 at 86. Her brother John was a well-known local contractor.

JULIA A. THYNNE, CLASS OF 1896. Julia was the daughter of immigrants Patrick and Catherine (O'Hara) and one of six children. Upon graduation from high school, she became a clerk in a shoe factory, and later a bookkeeper. She served as clerk of the Welfare Department from 1934 to 1947, and, later, as a bookkeeper for the Letoile Roofing Co. In her will she left a bequest for a "deserving girl graduate" of St. James High School to help pay for college tuition. Julia died in 1956.

HUGH DONAHUE, CLASS OF 1885.
Donahue, one of the city's most beloved doctors, was the son of Hugh and Julia Donahue. Hugh Sr. died from a heart attack at the age of 50 . After two years of high school, young Hugh went to work in a hat factory, then returned to complete his education. During his school and college years he was a baseball player, and was pitcher on the Sheridan A.C., one of the well-known clubs of his youth. He earned his medical degree at Harvard and set up a practice on Winter Street, later moved to White Street, and had his final office in his home at 187 Main Street. He was a specialist in children's diseases. Donahue was a charter member of the Elks. He died of a stroke in 1928 at the age of 63.

NELLIE JOSEPHINE MAGUIRE, CLASS OF 1896. Nellie was the daughter of John Maguire, an Irish-American, who was a prominent shoe manufacturer and the founder of the Fr. Matthew Total Abstinence Society. Nellie was a Society "belle" who had developed a reputation for her fine musical ability. In June 1900 she was wed to Dr. Hugh Donahue at a 7:30 a.m. service "in the presence of at least 1500 people." The reception was held at the Maguire home on Main Street complete with orchestra and an outdoor marquee under which refreshments were served. The Donahues had six children: twins Mary and Helen, John E., Frances Elinor, Nancy, and Jane. Nellie died in 1962 at 85 years of age.

MARGARET O'BRIEN, CLASS OF 1889. Margaret was the daughter of James O'Brien, who immigrated in 1872. Her mother, Katherine, was a Massachusetts native with an Irish father and a Nova Scotian mother. Margaret was a clerk-bookkeeper for numerous shoe firms. She also served as a bookkeeper for the Haverhill Trust Company. She did not marry but lived at the family home on 32 Auburn Street until moving to her sister Elizabeth's home on Westland Terrace. Margaret died in 1943.

ELIZABETH TERESA O'BRIEN, CLASS OF 1892. Elizabeth was the sister of Margaret, and one of the seven surviving children of James and Katherine O'Brien. She was a teacher for a few years after graduation, and in 1900 she married future Judge John J. Ryan (see p. 72). Their home was on the newly created Westland Terrace. The Ryans had two sons, John Jr. and Joseph, and a daughter, Elizabeth, who married James Molloy. Elizabeth O'Brien Ryan died in 1936.

MARY ALICE HINES, CLASS OF 1892. Mary Alice was the daughter of Patrick Hines, who immigrated in 1879, and ran a meat and provisions store at 240 Winter Street. Her mother was Augusta Kelly, a native of Boston. Patrick and Augusta married in 1866. In the 1900 Census, Patrick was listed as a widower and Mary Alice, who lived at home, as a school teacher. She continued to teach until 1904 when she married Thomas Aery.

ROSE G. FENNELLY, CLASS OF 1895. Rose was the daughter of Mark and Mary Fennelly, both Massachusetts-born of Irish parents. After high school, Rose worked as a clerk. The Fennellys lived at 7 Harrison Street. In 1900 the household included Rose's 68-year-old grandmother, Mary Harrington, who had immigrated in 1847. Rose married Lawrence Dunn, a veterinarian, and moved from the city.

MARY ALICE AND KATHERINE T. O'NEILL, CLASS OF 1895. The O'Neill twins were the daughters of James, a shoemaker who immigrated in 1865, and Mary E., who immigrated in 1868. James died before 1920 but his wife was still alive in 1930. Both of the twins became school teachers at the Winter Street School. Mary Alice disappears from the City Directory by 1920 but Katherine continues to be listed as a teacher and living at home through 1930. Their family home was at 15 Howard Street.

ELLEN C. SULLIVAN, CLASS OF 1895. "Nelly" lived at 27 High Street with her parents, Dennis and Bridget, both of who immigrated in 1855. Dennis was a day laborer. Nelly became a teacher at the Wingate School, in Lafayette Square, where her principal was Annie Roche. Nelly continued to teach at the Wingate School and to live at her family home through 1930.

CATHERINE HELEN REARDON, CLASS OF 1895. In the 1900 Census, Catherine is listed as living at 9 Rose Street with her widowed mother, the former Catherine Leonard, who had immigrated in 1860. Her father was John Reardon, a currier, who died of nephritis at Christmas time in 1891, aged 68. Catherine's mother died in 1901 and her sister Mary a year later. Catherine Helen was a teacher. She died in 1955.

CELIA RYAN, CLASS OF 1896. Celia was a clerk for various shoe companies. She was the daughter of Patrick and Ellen, an 1855 immigrant. They married in 1865, about the time that Patrick immigrated. The Ryans had 12 children, and in 1900 all 11 of the surviving children were living at home. Patrick was a dyer in the Stevens Woolen Mill on Hale Street, and his home at 8 Lewis Street was nearby. By 1920, Celia is listed in the City Directory as living with her brother Charles, a clerk in the post office, at 12 Dudley Street.

MARY F. FITZGERALD, CLASS OF 1896. Mary was the second of seven children born to James Fitzgerald, an 1867 immigrant who became a shoe manufacturer with his brother "P.J." Her mother was Mary A. O'Brien, who also immigrated in 1867. James had served as a state representative. The younger Mary went to the Haverhill Training School for Teachers and taught in local schools for almost 50 years. She retired from the Hannah Duston school in 1947 and died in 1950. Her brother was Attorney James Fitzgerald.

AGNES AUGUSTA BIRMINGHAM, CLASS OF 1896. Agnes lived with her widowed immigrant mother, Margaret, at 16 Lewis Street. Less than six months after graduating from high school, she married grocer Michael P. Fitzgerald, 15 years her senior. The 1900 Census notes that Agnes had the services of a 16-year-old servant to help her run her home at 39 Charles Street. The Fitzgeralds' son Harold was a policeman, and their daughter Connie worked for the city government. A third son, Edmund, moved to Illinois. Michael died in 1942, at age 80, and Agnes died nine years later.

KATHARINE R. MCCARTHY, CLASS OF 1888. The McCarthys lived on Park Avenue near Arch Avenue in the old Ward 5. The father, Patrick, an 1851 immigrant, was a hatter; the mother, Bridget, had immigrated in 1849. Daughter Katharine was one of two daughters to become Haverhill school teachers. She taught at the Winter Street School, and in 1910 was at the Wilson Street School, a small primary school near River and Beach Streets. She continued to teach throughout the 1920s. By 1930 she was living on Leroy Avenue in Bradford, and was still listed as a teacher.

ALICE MCCARTHY, CLASS OF 1893. Alice, the younger of the two teaching McCarthy sisters, had gone to the Teacher Training School on Portland Street after completing high school. In 1910, she was teaching at the Tilton School, where one of her colleagues was Teresa Roche, sister of Annie Roche. In 1920, she was listed as a stenographer for a business at 357 River Street, and in 1930, she was living with her sister Katharine on Leroy Avenue, but had no occupation listed.

MARY A. MURPHY, CLASS OF 1893. Mary's father, Patrick, had died in 1891 of pneumonia. He was 47 and was an assistant superintendent of the Gas House on Hilldale Avenue. Her mother, Johannah, who had immigrated in 1848, had ten children to raise. Mary attended the Teacher Training School and taught at the Monument Street and School Street Schools. By 1910, Mary's mother had purchased a home on 16th Avenue, and Mary A. was still teaching at the School Street School. That status was unchanged in 1920.

ROSE ETTA FAY, CLASS OF 1891. Rose Etta was born in Haverhill to Andrew Fay and his first wife, Ellen (Coughlin). Her father was a grocer and emigration agent, a city councillor in 1891 and 1892, and also served as sexton at St. James Church. The family lived over their store on Harrison Street until moving to Kenoza Avenue. Rose Etta taught for 44 years in Haverhill schools, first at the Currier and then the Burnham School. She was one of the founders of the Catholic Women's Club. She died in 1958 at the age of 85.

MAURICE L. MCCARTHY, CLASS OF 1897. Maurice, the younger brother of John and Michael (see p. 53), became a chemist. He finished Harvard College in only three years in 1900. A year later he received his master's degree in chemistry and stayed on to teach at Harvard for three years. He also taught at the Massachusetts Institute of Technology. Maurice went on to become a chemist for various companies in Jamaica and in Puerto Rico. He was married to Elinor Humphrey and, after retiring in 1930, returned to his family home on Maple Street. He died suddenly in 1952 at the age of 73.

JOHN H. MCCARTHY, CLASS OF 1895. John was one of three McCarthy brothers to graduate from Haverhill High School in the 1890s. Their father, Patrick, had died in 1891 at the age of 38 of phthisis, a severe form of consumption. Patrick had been a laborer, and the family lived in Bradford at the time of his death. His widow, Mary Maney, moved her family to "The Acre" to 30 Maple Street. John became a bookkeeper and eventually moved to Manchester, New Hampshire.

MICHAEL H. MCCARTHY, CLASS OF 1895. Michael worked in local shoe shops after graduation, as a shoe maker and as a stock fitter. He continued to live with his widowed mother at the Maple Street address. In 1920, he was listed as a foreman, and by 1930 he was a foreman for the Hartman Shoe Company and was listed as the owner of the house in which his mother still lived.

MICHAEL J. CRONIN, CLASS OF 1888. Michael was the son of Patrick, who immigrated in 1855, and Mary McCarty. They were both living in Georgetown when they married in 1857. And that is where Mary died in 1883, aged 51, of consumption. Patrick moved to Haverhill and was the coachman for G.A. Kimball of Mill Street. In 1900 Patrick was listed as living at 74 Summer Street with four Scandinavian boarders. He is not in the 1905 City Directory. Michael gave a recitation at his graduation. He became a shoemaker and by 1897 was living in his own home at 3 Driscoll Street.

WINIFRED M. POWERS, CLASS OF 1891. Winifred was the daughter of David and Margaret J., and their home was at 42 Mill Street. David was a shoemaker who was dead by 1900. Winifred attended the Teacher Training School on Portland Street and taught at the Whittier School (originally the Haverhill Academy) and the Locust Street School. By 1905, Winifred was listed as living at the Hotel Bartlett on Main Street with her sister Marguerite. They continued to be listed together through 1909. By 1910, Marguerite owned her own home at 54 Webster Street, but Winifred had disappeared from the City Directory.

FRANK M. LENNON, CLASS OF 1883.
Frank's parents, John Lennon and
Ellen Foley, had married in 1854.
John had died in 1880 at the age of
49. At that time the family lived on
Brickett Street in Riverside. Frank's
older brother, John, had his own
leather sole business, and by 1887 was
married to Mary A. Ryan, sister of
Celia (see p. 48). They moved to
Eighth Avenue. Frank was the first
member of his high school class to
die. He succumbed to consumption at
the age of 21 in 1886.

**MARGARET H.
LENNON, CLASS OF
1891.** Margaret, the
sister of Frank, lived
with her married
brother, John, on Eighth
Avenue while attending
Teacher Training
School and teaching at
the Currier School.
Margaret died in April
1894 before her 21st
birthday. Four months
later her mother, Ellen,
died of consumption,
the same disease that
had taken the life of her
son, Frank. Ellen was
aged 62.

DANIEL FRANK CALHANE, CLASS OF 1889. Frank Calhane's father, Daniel, owned a restaurant on Merrimack Street. The elder Calhane had emigrated from Ireland in 1858. His wife, Annie Emerson, was a native New Englander. Daniel Sr. died in 1919. The younger Daniel earned a bachelor's, master's, and doctorate in chemistry from Harvard. He died in 1951 after more than 30 years of distinguished teaching at Worcester Polytechnic Institute.

GRACE ANNIE CALHANE, CLASS OF 1893. The Calhane family home was at 58 Moore Street, off of Water Street. Grace became a teacher in the public schools, first at the Tilton Corner School in Riverside and later at the Kimball Street School in Bradford. She continued at that school through the 1920s. By 1930, she is listed as rooming at Claremont Avenue, but no occupation is listed.

JENNIE E. HANRAHAN, CLASS OF 1898. Jennie and her family emigrated from Ireland in 1881. Her parents had 13 children, but by 1900 only six were alive. Bridget died at 19 in 1885 of typhoid, Mary at 18 in 1888 of asthenia, and Julia at 14 in 1889 of an abscess of the brain. Nora, 28, and Annie, 26, died within days of each other in 1898 of consumption. And John, the father, died in 1896 at 45 of heart disease. After graduation Jennie worked as a shoe stitcher but eventually became a bookkeeper. She continued to live with her mother at 7 Lewis Street. By 1920 she had her own home at 18 White Street.

AGNES ANGELA HURLEY, CLASS OF 1896. The Hurleys emigrated from Co. Cork as a family. They arrived in 1880: father Timothy, a stone mason; mother Honoria; and the first five of the ten children the Hurleys would eventually have. Agnes became a school teacher after her graduation. In 1900 she was already a principal at the Monument Street School, a position she continued in for many years. In 1920, she is recorded as the principal of the Hannah Dustin School and a resident in her own home at 78 Columbia Park. She was the older sister of George and Augustine Hurley (see p. 31).

HENRY T. RYAN, CAPTAIN. Ryan was born in New Hampshire in 1855 of Irish parents. After moving to Haverhill, he was appointed a patrolman in 1882. He was promoted to Captain of the Night Watch by 1889, but that position was controlled by politics, and during a change in administration he was returned to the rank of patrolman. He retired in 1921. He lived at 43 North Street in the Acre with his wife, Catherine, and his four children.

MARCUS A. SULLIVAN, SERGEANT. The Sullivan home was at 40 North Broadway. John, the father, had emigrated from County Kerry in 1857. Abby, the mother, had arrived a year earlier. In 1900, they had been married for 39 years, and seven of their nine children were alive. Marcus was one of the middle children. He had been born in 1875 and appointed a patrolman in 1900. He was promoted to Sergeant in 1909. The 1910 Census lists him as living at 111 Main Street at the corner of Kenoza Avenue. By 1920 he was a captain in the police department. At that date his family home was at 4 South Williams Street, Bradford.

MICHAEL BRODERICK, PATROLMAN. Broderick had emigrated from Co. Limerick in 1888. He married Mary A. Keegan in 1896. She had immigrated in 1886. At the time of the wedding, Michael's occupation was a sole cutter. He was appointed a patrolman in 1897. By 1910, the family was living at 28 New Street, and Michael continued as a patrolman, a situation that remained constant in the 1920s and 1930s.

HERMAN McKENNA, PATROLMAN. Herman was born in Massachusetts to James and Mary McKenna, both of whom had emigrated from Ireland in 1853. They married in 1856. Herman, born in 1870, had trained as a pattern maker in the shoe industry. In 1904 he was appointed a patrolman. By 1910, he was married and living at 22 Dexter Street. The 1920 City Directory lists Herman as a sergeant and living at 126 Franklin Street. By 1930 he was deputy city marshall, and the family lived at 208 Franklin Street.

MICHAEL DONOGHUE, PATROLMAN. Donoghue immigrated in 1890. He had been born in 1858. Michael had been a special policeman in 1900 and was appointed a patrolman in 1904. By 1920, he is listed in the City Directory as being married to Margaret L. Donoghue, the daughter of Irish immigrants. They were living at 78 Haseltine Street in Bradford. He served as a pall bearer for James Bolan (see p. 61) as representative of the police department.

RICHARD GRIFFIN, DETECTIVE. Griffin was born on New Year's Day, 1880. His parents were Michael and Catherine (Welch) Griffin. His father had immigrated in 1869 and was a plasterer. His mother was dead by 1900. Richard was in the Class of 1898 at Haverhill High School but dropped out to go to work as a heel burnisher in the local shoe factories. In 1904, Herman McKenna persuaded Griffin to join him on the police force, and Griffin did regular beat work until 1912 when he passed the State Police examination and joined that force. Within a few years he had become a detective inspector working out of the Essex County District Attorney's office. He retired in 1945 but continued to work as a security officer while he pursued his favorite avocation of golf. He died in 1970 at the age of 90.

JOSEPH U. RYAN, PATROLMAN. Joseph Ryan's ancestors had emigrated from Ireland to Newfoundland and then on to Haverhill. His father, John F. Ryan, was born in Newfoundland, but his mother, Mary Hines, came from Ireland. They married on April 3, 1865. John was a brother to James Ryan, the father of "Scagey" Ryan. Mary Hines Ryan died in 1890, aged 48, of typhoid. John died in 1899. In the 1900 Directory, Joseph is listed as a boxmaker living with two sisters and a brother at 25 Blossom Street, Bradford. Ryan was appointed a patrolman in 1907. He was a sergeant by 1920 and living with wife Catherine at 75 Franklin Street. By 1930 they had moved to 429 Primrose Street.

JAMES BOLAN, PATROL DRIVER. Bolan was born in 1855 to one of Haverhill's pioneering Irish families. Tradition is that it was in the house of his parents, Thomas and Peggy Bolan on Hilldale Avenue, that the first Catholic Mass was said in Haverhill. Bolan was appointed to the police force in 1885. In 1906 he was named ambulance and patrol car driver. Bolan was a musician and an entertainer and an ardent member of the Elks. It was at an Elks picnic in 1921, just after he had finished performing for the crowd, that he suddenly died. He was 65 and was the first policeman in many years to have died in active service.

MICHAEL O'DONNELL, PATROLMAN. O'Donnell was an immigrant from Kilkenny, Co. Limerick. He immigrated in 1885, married Margaret Elizabeth Grace in 1893, and operated a grocery store on Locust Street with his brother Dennis. In 1906 he was appointed to the police force. The O'Donnell home was on River Street in Bradford. His wife died in 1917, and his oldest child, Fred, was killed in WW I in 1918 (see p. 88). By 1930, O'Donnell and his second wife, Elizabeth, were living at 7 Carleton Avenue in Bradford. Michael died suddenly at Christmas time in 1932, three weeks after his brother Dennis. Michael was 63.

DENNIS E. KELLEHER, PATROLMAN. Kelleher was born in Haverhill in 1884, the son of immigrants Jeremiah and Joanna (Shea) Kelleher. He was the brother of Dr. Edward, Dan, John, Annie, and "Toby" Kelleher. After attending the local parochial schools, he worked in shoe factories until his appointment to the force in 1909. He resigned in 1918 to return to the shoe business. During the 1920s he had his own business. He then became a district agent of the Shoe Workers Protective Union and later was an organizer for the C.I.O. shoe movement. He died of a heart attack in 1939 at the age of 55. He left a wife, Jennie Galvin, and two children, Bertha and Cornelius.

Four

THE PRE-WAR YEARS

D.J. CURTIN AND HIS MILK WAGON. Daniel J. Curtin had a milk delivery business between 1901 and 1908. His home was at 21 High Street during that time. He lived with his widowed father, Daniel. The elder Curtin had immigrated in 1875 from Co. Limerick. He was a foreman in the City Street Department and a ready source of employment to his fellow countrymen. His wife, Hannah Falvey, had died of breast cancer in 1899. Her youngest child was eight. By 1910, the younger Daniel had his own house at 3 Cottage Street, where he lived with his three sisters and one brother. All were unmarried. Dan had given up the milk business and was employed as a teamster. The elder Daniel, in the meantime, had married widow Nora Costello, adopted her daughter Mary, and had a daughter Florence.

JEREMIAH LYNCH AND SON GEORGE. Jeremiah Lynch was a teamster for the Taylor-Goodwin Lumber Company, located by the Merrimack River in the Lower End of Bradford. He had emigrated from Co. Cork in 1890. He married Bridget Leary in 1893 and they had seven children. He is shown here, in 1908, with his young son George. In later years, George married Madeline Dacey, daughter of Pat and Hanna Dacey (see p. 16).

JORDAN'S IRISH JAUNTING CART. Jim Jordan, baker, decided to add some Irish touches to his new home in Haverhill, so he imported a jaunting cart. Henry Ford later bought the cart for his new museum in Michigan, but he eventually decided against displaying it because it did not fit his criterion of being made in America. Jordan is shown here at the corner of Winter and Vine Streets. In the rear can be seen the new Hibernian building where the YMCA now stands. Seated in front are daughters Rose and Rita Jordan and Jim's niece, Mary Lysaght. Behind them are his niece, Kate Howard, Jordan, and his daughter Mary.

JORDAN'S STORE, PRIMROSE STREET. Jim Jordan, born in Co. Clare, Ireland, in 1870, came to Haverhill early in the 1900s. He opened a bakery on Winter Street with outlets on Washington Street and Lafayette Square. Each Monday morning he would deliver his leftover baked goods to families in the Acre, which inspired a local poet to rhyme: "Jim Jordan the Baker, Feeds the kids in the Acre, Keeps them all from the undertaker." After the family moved to 206 Primrose Street, he opened a small grocery store there, operated by his wife. Mary Jordan came from London, England. She is shown here with three of her sons and an unidentified clerk.

JORDAN'S GLOBE CAFE. James Jordan opened his restaurant, the Globe Cafe, at 47 Locust Street about 1907. It continued in business until the early 1930s. This photo was taken in 1914. Behind the counter are Jordan's niece, Mary Lysaght, newly arrived from Ireland, and his daughter Mary. Jim Jordan had one final business venture. With money he had won in the Irish Sweepstakes, he built three cottages at Salisbury Beach. Jordan died in 1932, aged 62.

WINTER STREET BAKERY WAGON. Patrick Lysaght was a nephew of Jim Jordan and a brother to Mary Lysaght. He immigrated, with his uncle's help, in 1908 when he was 17 years old. He drove a bakery wagon for his uncle and boarded with his family.

ON THE BEACH. Whether American born or Irish born, young men enjoy showing off at the beach. Young immigrant Pat Lysaght demonstrates his perfect balance and tries to attract some attention, as he stands on the shoulders of his friend Tim Dempsey.

THE BURKE FAMILY. William "Billy" Burke, born in So. Groveland, married Rose Finnin of Haverhill in 1897. Both were the children of immigrants. Billy was a pioneer in promoting bicycling and bicycle racing. He manufactured the Pentucket bicycle and owned shops on Water Street, Locust Street, and in the Hibernian Building on Winter Street. Burke was an active member of the Knights of Columbus, the Hibernians, and the Elks. Billy and Rose had three children, William and Mildred, shown here, and Rose.

BILLY BURKE'S PENTUCKET BICYCLE STORE. Billy Burke operated a number of stores, including this one in Schenectady, New York. All of the stores carried much more than bicycles, including typewriters and phonographs, all "cutting edge" technology in the early 1900s. Billy is shown on the right. He died at the age of 44 in 1916.

THE CRONINS' DELIVERY HORSE. When James Cronin (see p. 9) left his job at a local tannery, he opened a grocery store in his home on Kimball Street. Neighborhood grocers delivered to their customers, so a horse was a necessity. Three of the Cronin boys and two chums pose with "Old Dobbin." Pictured from left to right are (front row) Jim Cronin and Pat and James Somers; (back row) Frank and Bill Cronin.

ROLL OUT THE BARRELS! In the days before everything came pre-packaged in a grocery store, the goods arrived in barrels. Frank and Jim Cronin sit astride two such barrels at the rear of their father's store. In later years, Frank worked for the Gas Company, and Jim was a policeman.

FOOTBALL, IRISH STYLE. There were so many young Irish immigrants in Haverhill by the turn of the century that they could carry on many of their native sports such as Gaelic football. Four of these young men have been identified. They are the Hoar brothers, who came from County Kerry with their parents and other family members. This helps to date the picture to about 1910. In the back row from left to right are Patrick, Thomas, unidentified, Michael, and Jack Hoar. Others are unidentified.

JOHN W. DWYER, BAND LEADER. John Dwyer had emigrated from Canada as a child in 1874. He was a musician and a music teacher, as well as director of the Haverhill Brass Band. The Brass Band was just one of many musical organizations in the city at a time when people still made their own entertainment. Even organizations, such as the Foresters, had their own orchestra. The phonographs that Billy Burke was selling would soon present a serious challenge to local amateur and professional music-making.

69

THE ROCHE FAMILY AT SALISBURY BEACH, 1912. David Roche was a leading figure in Haverhill's Irish community. His Roche parents, grandparents, aunts, and uncles had immigrated to the city in the early 1850s from Co. Kerry. His uncle John was the first Irish city councillor. His father, James, was a grocer. David was a superintendent at the Pentucket (Stevens textile) Mills for over 40 years. He was also an alderman and school committee member, as well as chairman of the Democratic City Committee. As with so many of the upwardly mobile Irish-Americans of the early 20th century, the family spent their summer vacation at the beach. Pictured from left to right are Mary, Dolly, Faber, and Donald Roche; Evelyn Costello; David and Mary Jane (Dorsey) Roche; Joe Gavin; Nan and Bernadette Roche; Catherine "Cass" Quimby; and Katherine Roche.

ROCHES AT THE BEACH, 1914. Pictured from left to right are (front) Liza McPhee; Katherine, Nan, Bernadette, and Mary Roche; unidentified, Aunt Mayme Roche; Aunt "Maggo" Roche; and Dolly Roche; (rear) Dave, Mary Jane, Faber, and Donald Roche; Ben Belken; Leo Roche and Dave's brother Bill Roche with daughter Mary; and Joe Gavin (son of Dennis and Bridget), who married Bernadette Roche.

FORESTERS CHIEF RANGERS. Merrimack Court of Foresters, a fraternal and mutual help organization, celebrated its 25th anniversary in 1913. Eleven of its 12 first Chief Rangers were present and posed for this picture. They are from left to right (front) John J. or Timothy W. Murphy, Daniel Maguire (businessman and brother of John E.), Richard Dwyer (a hatter and first Ranger), and David Roche (see p. 70); (rear) Thomas Bough (former alderman, father of policeman Tom, and schoolteacher Mary), John O'Brien (brother of Margaret and Elizabeth, p. 45, and a court officer), John Burns (see p. 28), John T. Desmond (architect, city engineer, and alderman), and John E. (former alderman) and John J. or Timothy W. Murphy. The only missing Ranger was Bernard Haughey (see p. 25), who had died in 1910.

Joseph and John Ryan Jr. These two boys with their dappled gray horse were the sons of Judge John Ryan (see p. 112) and Elizabeth O'Brien (see p. 45). The photo was taken in 1908 when Joseph was about four and John Jr. was six. The family home was on Westland Terrace near Lake Saltonstall. Joe died when he was 11. John Ryan Jr. went to Holy Cross and Harvard Law School. He joined his father in his law practice in 1928. He was appointed assistant district attorney in 1931 and served in that position for 20 years. Ryan had just received one of the highest honors in his field, being named a Fellow of the American College of Trial Lawyers, when he died suddenly in 1962. He was 60 years old and left four children: Mary, Angela, John III, and Joseph.

THOMAS AND MARY KEATING KELLY.
Thomas Kelly, born in 1838 in Lisbride, Co. Roscommon, married Mary Keating in the mid-1860s in Roscommon. Mary was born in 1848. They immigrated to America after their nine children were born, and they settled in South Groveland. They were drawn there, as were many Irish, by the work available in the textile mill. The strong presence of the Irish was reflected in the name (St. Patrick's) and the location (So. Groveland) given to the new Catholic parish in Groveland. Thomas died in 1916, and Mary died in 1928.

MARY KELLY AND PATRICK MALYNN.
Mary Kelly was the second daughter of Thomas and Mary Keating Kelly. She was born in Roscommon in 1877. Mary married Patrick J. Malynn about 1906. She died in 1937 at the age of 60 just before Christmas. She is shown with her five sons on page 99 about that time. Patrick was also born in Co. Roscommon. He was 14 when he arrived in Portland, Maine, on his way to meet his brothers and sisters in Boston. When the Malynns were first married they lived in West Roxbury but soon moved to 358 Primrose Street, where they raised their family. Patrick died in 1961 at the age of 87.

73

SAINT JAMES SCHOOL 25TH REUNION, 1912. St. James Parish celebrated the 25th anniversary of the opening of its parish school with a grand banquet on January 30, 1912. The location was St. Patrick's Hall in the high school building. Immediately facing the camera are Jerome Burke (see p. 31), Teresa Griffin, Hazel Sullivan, Richard Griffin (see p. 60), Agnes Moynihan, Florence Moran, Hannah O'Connell, Katherine Ring, Rebecca Carey, Agnes Donovan (all of the Class of 1911), and Madeline Dacey (see p. 64). Facing the camera at the third table in are, from the right, Dr. and Mrs. Hugh Donahue, John Maguire, and David Roche.

JEREMIAH AND DANIEL MINIHAN. Timothy Minihan, born in Co. Cork in 1872, immigrated to Haverhill in 1901. Soon after, he married Nora Duggan from Co. Kerry. Their first child, Jeremiah, was born in 1903. Their second child, also a son, Daniel, was born two years later. Jerry gave up a promising athletic career to become a priest. He rose to the rank of Bishop (see p. 121). Danjo became a lawyer and an alderman for the City of Haverhill (see p. 125). Nora died in 1947, Danjo in 1949, Timothy in 1962, and Bishop Jeremiah in 1973. This picture was probably taken at the boys' First Communion, as suggested by the white bows they are wearing on their arms.

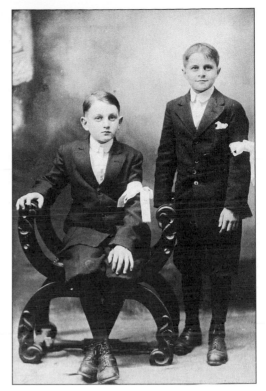

SONNY AND KATE MAHONEY. William Mahoney was born in Araglen, Co. Cork, in 1884. The family tradition is that he was caught poaching salmon and escaped to America to avoid prosecution by the local landlord. He immigrated in 1897. His sister Nora, born in 1878, preceded him, immigrating in 1895. In 1900 she was a servant at 32 Webster. She married Edward Fitzgerald, a bartender, in 1905. In 1910, the Fitzgeralds, one child, and William Mahoney, a shoe cutter, were all living together at 88 Sixth Avenue. "Sonny" Mahoney married Catherine "Kate" Linehan in 1912. Kate was one of many Linehans who had come from the area around Abbeyfeale, Co. Limerick. The Mahoneys had seven children, one of whom died young. Kate died in 1969 and "Sonny" died a year later, in 1970.

75

THE SHAMROCKS A.C. The Shamrocks Athletic Club was an organization of young men, principally from "the Acre." They sponsored both a basketball and a baseball team that took part in city-wide competition. They were founded in 1910. The members are shown here at their 1912 banquet.

ANNIE FITZGERALD. The beautiful Annie Josephine Fitzgerald was the daughter of Johannah (see p. 14) and John Dennis Fitzgerald. She was born in Bradford in 1888. The family moved to 75 Fifth Avenue in 1896. Her brother Donal (later Daniel) was born in 1890. He married Edith Coakley. A sister Catherine died young. Two other siblings, Margaret and John Francis, did not marry. In 1920, Florence "Florry" Sullivan purchased a house at 79 Fifth Avenue, next door to the Fitzgeralds, and a year later married Annie Josephine. They had two children, Helen who maintains the family home, and James, a realtor on Cape Cod.

76

THE HOAR FAMILY. Michael and Ellen (Quirk) Hoar came to Haverhill from Annascaull, Co. Kerry. From left to right are (front) Helen (Mrs. J. Henry Woelflein), Mary (Mrs.—Curtin), Michael Hoar, Ellen Quirk Hoar, Bridget (Mrs. John J. Sullivan), and Margaret (Mrs. Frank Glidden); (rear) Patrick, John, Michael, and Thomas Hoar. Mary was the first to arrive, in 1895 when she was 15. Bridget arrived next in 1898 when she was 14. Both girls were employed as domestics. Michael Sr. immigrated in 1900, the year his wife gave birth to their eighth child, Helen or "Nellie." The rest of the family came in 1905. The photo was taken about 1910 when the family was living at 5 Marshall Street. Michael was a laborer for the Street Department, John and Thomas were shoemakers, Patrick a helper, and the others still in school. Michael, the father, died in 1919.

PEASLEE BOYS REUNION. The "Old Peaslee Boys" was another informal organization of young men, like the Shamrocks. The name came from Peaslee's Crossing, Newton, New Hampshire, where the young men, primarily from the "Acre," would go. Supposedly, they would ride the electric cars from downtown Haverhill to that rural location to "hang out" at a local inn. They also sponsored a wide range of athletic events, including bowling tournaments. The program for their 1916 banquet was probably typical. Police Officer James Bolan, "master of the Canadian dialect," and James "Scagey" Ryan delivered monologues. Dick Barry played the piano, and Bill and Joe Gavin sang. Dennis Kelleher was the chairman of the committee. All are names that have appeared previously in this volume.

SAINT JAMES HIGH SCHOOL, CLASS OF 1913. From left to right are (front row) William Barron, Esther Melody (see p. 24), D. Raymond Moynihan (see p. 86), Helen Fennelly, and Harry Buckley; (second row) Cora Gaudette, Dorothy Lennon (see p. 120), Elizabeth Lane, Edith McGovern, Irene Carey, Agnes Murphy, Helen Hussey, and Catherine Somers; (third row) Maurice Heffernan, Marie Bousfield, Elizabeth Sullivan, Mary Dacey (see p. 16), Mary Mellon, Katherine McNamara, Gertrude Keene, and Edward Callaghan; (fourth row) Daniel O'Leary, J. Alva Burns (see p. 90), John Fitzpatrick, Joseph A. Kelly, John Cummings (see p. 85), Joseph Creed, and Timothy Ring.

SAINT JAMES HIGH SCHOOL, CLASS OF 1915. From left to right are (front row) Lillian Wright, C. Frank Linnehan, Dolly Roche (see p. 70), John McNamara, Catherine Coddaire, John Lane (see p. 17), and Grace Kelly; (second row) Cecile Gilbert, Marie Purcell, Alexina Morel, Carlene Shevenel, Antoinette Buckley, Georgianna Bousfield, and Alice Carragher; (third row) Anna Quintal, Gertrude Carey, Florence Conley, Agatha Costello, Josephine McBride, Marion Callahan, Alice Dorsey (see p. 35), and Mary Sullivan; (fourth row) Lott McNamara, Luke Richards, Lawrence McCarthy, Anthony Ryan (see p. 107), Harold Fitzgerald (see p. 128), Joseph Herlihy (see p. 113), William Garvey, and Harold Ryan.

AUSTIN HAYES, INDUSTRIAL AND CIVIC LEADER. Austin Hayes was born in 1883 to immigrants Cornelius and Julia Hayes. He had three sisters. Though his father died before Austin had finished Haverhill High School, he was able to go on to M.I.T., where he studied chemistry. He put his scientific knowledge to good advantage when he went to work for Lennox and Briggs, a major leather tanning company in Haverhill. Austin rose to the rank of vice-president before he was 40 years old. He also found time to lead the Elks and the Pentucket Club, to be an outstanding golfer, and to be a director of two local banks. He and his family made their home at 12 Fernwood Avenue, Bradford. He died suddenly in 1930 at the age of 47.

HELEN MARTIN HAYES. Helen was the daughter of Walter and Janice Martin. After graduating from Haverhill High School and the Garland Kindergarten School, Boston, she married Austin Hayes. After his death in 1930, she returned to teaching. Helen was on the staff of the Tilton School for many years. The Hayes had five children: Austin, Richard, John, Mary (Mrs. Paul) Bresnahan, and Anne (Mrs. Thomas) Dorsey. Helen died in 1962.

Five

WAR, AND WAR AGAIN!

THE HORGAN FAMILY IN WORLD WAR II. Many with Irish pedigrees gave their lives in WW I and lie buried in French soil. Just as many fell victim to the horrendous influenza epidemic of 1918–19, which made its first appearance in American military bases. Twenty-three years later, another world-wide conflict witnessed another generation of Irish-Americans offer their service, and their lives, to their country. This time, those that made the ultimate sacrifice were buried around the globe. Above are the Horgans, the sons and daughter of Irish immigrants Patrick and Mary (O'Connor), all of whom survived the war. In front are Donnell, who served in both the European and Pacific battle zones for 23 months; Mary, a WAVE; and Raymond, who earned seven battle stars during 27 months in the Pacific. In back are Paul, who, as a member of the Counter Intelligence Corps, helped capture Tokyo Rose; Robert, a member of the Air Corps, who spent 33 months in the Pacific; Patrick, who served in an army medical unit and was later a city councilor in Haverhill; and Allen, who served 29 months overseas in the Army Air Corps in both the European and Pacific battle zones.

CORPORAL JAMES DANIEL CONLEY. Conley was the son of Thomas and Margaret (McAuliffe) of 41 Fourth Avenue. Both were the children of immigrants. Thomas was a superintendent in a shoe factory. James was a member of the Quartermaster Corps at Fort Devens, where he died of pneumonia on September 24, 1918. In 1918, "death by pneumonia" usually indicated a victim of the great influenza epidemic.

CORPORAL JEREMIAH J. CRONIN. Cronin had been born in Malden to Dennis and Mary (Sullivan). He moved to Haverhill where he was a letter carrier and an active member of the Knights of Columbus and the Fr. Matthew Society. He joined the Army as a 30 year old in June 1918, and he was sent to Wentworth Institute for training. He was stricken with pneumonia while sailing to France and died in a hospital in Bourdeaux, France, on October 5, 1918.

CORPORAL DANIEL FRANCIS COOPER. Cooper was the son of William and Minnie Etta (Sullivan). In the 1910 Census, his mother is listed as a widow and living at 51 Stewart Street. Daniel enlisted as a member of Company E, 23rd U.S. Infantry in March 1917. He was killed in action in Parroy, France, in June 1918. He was 25 years old. He was a first cousin of Private Daniel Sullivan (below) and the nephew of Daniel and Nora Sullivan (see p. 20).

PRIVATE DANIEL JOSEPH SULLIVAN. Daniel was the son of William Sullivan, a brother to Minnie Etta Sullivan Cooper, and Theresa (Young). William had immigrated in 1868 as an infant. He was a mason. In 1910, Theresa was listed as a widow and living at 89 Franklin Street. Daniel was one of three brothers in the service. He had enlisted in the Army on September 6, 1918. He died of pneumonia in Syracuse, New York, 20 days later, September 26, 1918.

CORPORAL JOHN FRANCIS COUGHLIN. John was the son of John and Mary (Mahoney), both of whom had immigrated in the mid-1880s. They married in 1893, and their son John was born three years later. Their home was at 28 Lewis Street. Young John was a member of Battery A, 102nd U.S. Field Artillery. He enlisted in March 1917 and was killed in action in France in October 1918.

PRIVATE PHILIP PATRICK MCMURRER. McMurrer, born in Haverhill in 1897, was the son of Irish immigrants Hugh and Delia (Madden). Hugh was a box maker, and the family home was at 1 Rose Avenue. Philip enlisted in July 1917 and was a member of a Machine Gun Battalion. He was killed in action in France in July 1918. McMurrer Park in the "Acre" is named in his honor.

3RD CLASS FIREMAN JOHN J. CUMMINGS. Cummings was born in Haverhill in 1896 to John and Elizabeth (Hughes). Both of his parents were born in Wales of Irish parents. Their home was on Blossom Street in Bradford. John Sr. was a janitor at the Moody School and very active in the Foresters. Young John, who enlisted in May 1918, was stationed at Newport, Rhode Island, and died in Haverhill of pneumonia in October 1918. He was a member of the Class of 1913 at St. James High School.

LIEUTENANT PATRICK ALEXANDER FINNEGAN. Finnegan was born in Newburyport, but his family was living on So. Kimball Street, Bradford, by 1910. His parents were born in Ireland and both immigrated in the 1880s. His father, John, was an engineer at the Haverhill Boxboards. His mother was Julia Burke. Patrick, who enlisted in July 1918, was commissioned a second lieutenant, assigned as an instructor to Temple University in Philadelphia. He died in that city in October 1918 of pneumonia. The square by Bradford Common is named in his honor.

PRIVATE JEREMIAH E. MOYNIHAN. Moynihan was the son of Daniel and Ellen (McCarthy), who had emigrated from Ireland in the mid-1870s. They married in 1888, and Jeremiah was born in 1893. The family lived at 3 York Street, and Daniel was a morocco dresser (leather worker). Jeremiah was a member of Battery A, 102nd U.S. Field Artillery. He died of appendicitis at Hale Hospital, Haverhill, in May 1917. He was the first member of Battery A to die. Among his siblings was the future Msgr. D. Raymond Moynihan (see p. 78).

PRIVATE HERBERT T. SLATTERY. Slattery was the son of Daniel, a Haverhill native, and Nora (Sheehan), who emigrated from Ireland in 1884. The Slatterys married in 1890, and Herbert was born in 1892. The family lived at 17 Burke Street, where Daniel was night watchman for the Haverhill railroad depot. In 1918, Nora was listed as a widow who supported her family as a shoe worker. Herbert had enlisted in May 1918. He died in France of pneumonia in September 1918 and is buried there.

COLOR SERGEANT MICHAEL DONAHUE NOONAN. Noonan was Haverhill's only Irish immigrant to die during WW I. He was a career man serving as a member of the Headquarters Company 11th U.S. Infantry. Michael was born in Ballyporeen, County Tipperary, in 1869 the son of Dennis and Johanna (Donahue). He was a brother to Patrick Noonan (see p. 21). Noonan enlisted in 1897 and served in Cuba, the Philippines, and the Mexican border. He went to France in April 1918. Color Sergeant Noonan died of organic heart trouble in Limoges, France, in October 1918 and is buried in the American Cemetery there.

CORPORAL FRED O'DONNELL. O'Donnell was born in Haverhill in 1894 to Michael and Margaret E. (Grace). His father was a police officer (see p. 62), who had immigrated to Haverhill in 1885. His mother had been born in Vermont of Irish parents. Fred was a member of Co. G, 16th U.S. Infantry. He had enlisted in 1915. O'Donnell was killed in action in France in July 1918. Central Square in Bradford honors his memory.

PRIVATE LEO EDWARD SULLIVAN. Leo was born in Haverhill in 1898. His father, Patrick, had immigrated in 1886 and was a railroad gate tender. His mother, Catherine (Donovan), had immigrated in 1872 as a child. The family lived at 30 Stewart Street. Leo had enlisted in Co. F, 104th U.S. Infantry in February 1917. He was killed in action in France in October 1918.

CORPORAL ADRIAN McLAUGHLIN. McLaughlin was the son of William Patrick McLaughlin and Rose Carter. He was born in Haverhill in 1894. His father was a shoe manufacturer, and, in 1918, the family house was on exclusive Windsor Street. Adrian had been a member of a Motor Truck Company. He died in France, October 20, 1918, just weeks before the war ended. The cause of death was pneumonia.

FRANCIS COTTER, VETERAN. Hundreds of Irish-American young men served in WW I. Most survived. Francis Cotter was the son of Jack and Minnie (Sullivan) (see page 23). He was born in 1900 and had worked as a clerk. Cotter enlisted in the U.S. Navy during the war. Unfortunately, he contracted tuberculosis during his term of service and spent years in hospitals until his death in 1933.

PATRICK MALONE, VETERAN. Malone, who was born in 1890, was a 1914 immigrant from Prince Edward Island, Canada. He was a descendant of Irish immigrants to that maritime province. He had served in the medical corps at Fort Ethan Allen, Vermont, for just two months when the November 11 Armistice was declared. Patrick worked in wood heel shops as a civilian. He married Katherine McCloskey and had nine children, four of whom entered the religious life. He died in 1974. His wife Katherine died in 1983.

JOSEPH ALVA BURNS, SAILOR. J. Alva Burns, on the right standing, was the son of John and Frances Burns (see p. 28). He was born in 1897 and had worked as a newsboy while going to school. He graduated from St. James High School in 1913 (see p. 78). Burns served in the U.S. Navy as a Gunner on the Scout Patrol, City of Lewis. He was employed after the war as a wood heeler, and he died suddenly in New York City in 1926 while on business, leaving behind wife Rosetta and baby daughter Hilda.

DENNIS F. DONOVAN, SAILOR.
Dennis was the son of Andrew
Donovan and Katie Donovan,
immigrants who married in 1896.
Dennis was born in 1900. His
mother died unexpectedly in 1905,
and Dennis was raised by relatives.
He joined the Navy during the last
year of WW I. He died in 1939.

EUGENE WALTER MELODY, VETERAN. Walter was
the first-born son of Michael, born in England of
Irish parents, and Margaret (Callaghan) (see p. 24),
an Irish immigrant. He served in the Army in
Battery A and returned safely to civilian life. He
died in 1969.

BOATSWAIN RICHARD DALY. Daly was the son of Richard and Melida. He had enlisted in the Navy during WW I at the age of 15. When that war ended he joined the Merchant Marine and continued with that service through WW II. He was killed in 1944. His convoy had been attacked, and, though his ship remained afloat, Daly was part of a rescue party to help others. The rescue party was attacked and killed.

CORPORAL JOSEPH DAVID FITZGERALD. Joseph was the son of David Joseph and Grace (Dougherty) Fitzgerald. He was born in 1915, and three years later his father died leaving his mother a widow. Joe graduated from Groveland High School. He enlisted in the Army in 1942 and spent the next two years stateside. Fitzgerald was sent to France in 1944 as a jeep driver and was killed there in December 1944. He is buried in France. He left a widow Gladys and son David.

SERGEANT JOHN J. HEFFERAN JR.
Hefferan was the grandson of Irish
immigrants. His parents, Mr. and Mrs.
John Hefferan Sr., lived on 19 Lamoille
Avenue in Bradford. He graduated
from Haverhill High School in 1941.
Hefferan enlisted in 1942 and was in
training as a bottom-turret gunner in a
B-17 airplane. In 1943, while on a
night training mission, his plane
crashed, and all aboard were killed.

PFC FREDERICK D. NOONAN. Noonan
was the son of David and Delia
Noonan. David Noonan, a WW I
veteran, had emigrated from Ireland in
1909. He died in 1940. His son,
Frederick, had gone overseas in
December 1944 and in the few
remaining months of war saw service in
Holland, Belgium, and Germany. He
fought during the German winter
offensive in the Ardennes and at the
Battle of the Colmar Pocket in Alsace,
France, when the Germans were driven
back across the Rhine River. Noonan
was killed in April 1945 while his
division was clearing the Germans from
the Ruhr Pocket. He is buried in a
military cemetery in Holland.

LIEUTENANT EVERETT J. CARNEY. Carney was the son of immigrants John and Mary (Garrity). His three older brothers, Francis, William, and Louis, had served in WW I. Everett graduated from Haverhill High School in 1925 and from the Wentworth Institute, where he was trained as an engineer. He entered the service in August 1941, before Pearl Harbor, and was sent to the Philippines where he directed construction of Clark Field on Luzon. When the Japanese captured the Philippine Islands, Carney was taken a prisoner and forced into the infamous Bataan Death March. He died in September 1942 and is buried in the Philippines.

PFC PATRICK O'BRIEN. Pat O'Brien had attended St. James High School and had played semi-professional baseball. He entered the Army in 1942 and saw extended service in the Pacific Theater of Operations. He was in New Caledonia and Guadalcanal before being sent to the Fiji Islands, where he was killed in a truck accident. O'Brien was the adopted son of William "Sikes" O'Brien, a scrap leather dealer noted for his many philanthropies, and Catherine (Goodman), an Irish immigrant.

CADET JOSEPH F. O'BRIEN JR. O'Brien's home was at 438 South Main Street, Bradford. He had graduated from Haverhill High School in 1943 and enlisted in the Air Corps. Joseph had completed his pilot training and was three weeks from graduation when his plane crashed during a thunder storm in Indiana. He had earned his wings, which were sent home to his parents, Joseph and Lillian O'Brien.

CAPTAIN WILLIAM D. GLYNN. Bill Glynn may have been Haverhill's most well-known fatality during WW II, for his father was the city's mayor. Albert W. Glynn (see p. 124) held that position longer than any other mayor in the city's history. Glynn's mother was Rosetta McDonald. Young Glynn had graduated from the Naval Academy at Annapolis in 1942 and received his commission in the Marines. He fought throughout the South and Central Pacific. He was killed while attempting a beachhead on the island of Guam in July 1944.

PFC JOSEPH E. LEVIS. Joseph Levis was the youngest child of former alderman and grocer Samuel Levis, the son of Irish immigrants, and of Mary Cronin. The family lived on 19 Rosedale Avenue. Young Levis graduated from St. James High School in 1934. He entered the Army in 1942 and was trained as a navigator for the Army Air Corps. He was killed during a routine flight in Kansas in August 1945, just days before the war ended.

LIEUTENANT WILLIAM F. GAVIN. Gavin was born in Haverhill, the son of Joseph and Bernadette (Roche) (see p. 70). He was the grandson of Dennis and Bridget Gavin (see p. 18) and David and Ann (Dorsey) Roche (see p. 70). He graduated from Haverhill High School in 1935 and enlisted in the Army Air Corps in 1940. He was first assigned to ferry bombers to Hawaii. Later, he received his wings and became a B-17 pilot. He took part in several missions over Germany. Gavin's plane crashed on June 11, 1944, soon after D-Day.

Lieutenant Harold J. Lafey.
Lafey had entered the Navy in 1919 and had earned retirement by 1936. When the war broke out in Europe, he was recalled to duty. He was assigned to a variety of ships that fought on the Atlantic, including the USS *Moffet,* which hosted a secret meeting between President Roosevelt and Prime Minister Churchill. His destroyer, the USS *Meredith,* was protecting troop ships to Normandy two days after D-Day when his ship struck a mine. His father, John Lafey, was the son of Irish immigrants, and his mother, Mary Quinn, was a native of Ireland.

Seaman 1/c Patrick F. Linehan.
Patrick Linehan was born in 1925 to Patrick (see p. 122) and Mary (Cash). He attended St. James High School and enlisted in the Navy in 1943. He was trained as an armed guard for merchant marine ships. His ship, the SS *John Harvey*, had been sent to North Africa and then on to Italy. While anchored in Bari Harbor, Italy, in December 1943, German planes attacked his ship, which was loaded with high explosives. His death was not officially confirmed until two years later.

S/Sgt. David Roche Gavin and Co-Pilot. Gavin, right, was the brother of William Gavin and had enlisted in the Air Corps at the same time. He was assigned to the Burma-India-China area to fly materials into China. His plane had been shot down over Burma in July 1943, and Gavin and the crew had been lost for 16 days and were presumed dead before being found by native Burmese and reunited. He is shown in the photo with his co-pilot, Lt. John Van Derver, in Kunming, China. After the war, David married Marian Hoar, daughter of Patrick and Mary (Lysaght) Hoar (see p. 105).

The Malynn Brothers. All five of the sons of Patrick and Mary (Kelly) Malynn (see p. 73), of Primrose Street, served their country in one form or another during WW II. Anthony ("Narky"), Mike, and Tom all fought in Europe with the Army. "Narky" received a Purple Heart with Oak Leaf Cluster. John was also in the Army, and Pat Jr. worked at the Charlestown Navy Yard. Pictured from left to right are (front) Pat Jr., mother Mary, and Michael; (rear) Thomas, John, and Anthony.

CORPORAL BERNARD "BARNEY" GALLAGHER. In what would be a portent of his future, "Barney" is shown with his camera. More than 50 years later, he is the dean of Haverhill newsmen after a career as reporter, editor, and columnist. He no longer straps on a pistol, but a camera is still close at hand. Barney was the son of James, a Canadian immigrant, and Mary Butler, whose parents had come from Ireland. He had begun work as a news photographer while still a student at Haverhill High School. He entered the Army in 1942 and served in the Pacific as a military photographer. When the war ended, he married Gladys, widow of Corporal Joseph Fitzgerald.

Six

BETWEEN THE WARS

TIMOTHY O'DRISCOLL AND KIMBALL CLEMENT. Timothy O'Driscoll was born in 1893 in Lissacaha, Parish of Schull, Co. Cork. He sailed from Queenstown (later Cobh), Cork, in January 1921 and settled in Haverhill. He was employed by Kimball Clement, descendant of one of Haverhill's oldest families, to care for Clement's horses and his pack of beagles. Tim is shown with Clement and the beagles. Driscoll (the "O" seems to have disappeared) married Helen Ring, from Moulagow, Co. Kerry, in 1926. They had two sons. Timothy died in 1938 while still employed by Clement, and Helen died in 1982.

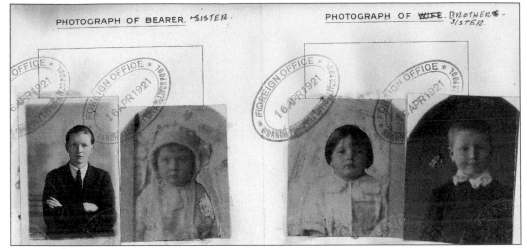

PHOTOGRAPH OF BEARER. *SISTER*.

PHOTOGRAPH OF ~~WIFE~~. *BROTHERS*. *SISTER*.

FOYNES CHILDREN. These are the passport photos of John Foynes and his baby sister Frances. They were natives of Kilmallock, Co. Limerick. Frances was born in 1916. While she was a young child, her parents died within two weeks of each other during the great influenza epidemic. In 1921, her brother John Foynes, who had gone to America to find a home for his family, returned to bring Frances, her brother Gerard, and sister Claire to America. They lived in Haverhill with their aunt and uncle, William and Bridget Moynihan. Then, when Frances was 15, her aunt and uncle died, and the Foynes children separated. Frances still managed to graduate from St. James High School in 1935. Two years later, she married Romeo Emilio, the son of Italian immigrants. They had twin daughters, Claire (Mrs. Richard Wilson) and Romaine (Mrs. Donald Shea). Frances became a citizen in 1946, and she died in 1984.

JEREMIAH AND MARGARET McCARTHY MURPHY. Jerry McCarthy was born in Ballybawn East, Ballydehob, Co. Cork, in 1903. Margaret McCarthy was born in Ballinlough, Parish of Leap, Co. Cork, in 1907. Both immigrated to Haverhill after Ireland won its independence. Jerry worked for the Haverhill Gas Company, and Margaret was a domestic. They were married by 1938, had two sons, William J.F. and John J., and lived at 34 So. Chestnut Street in Bradford. The Murphys, like many of the post-WW I Irish immigrants, were able to make many trips back to their native homes. After WW II, Margaret helped numerous McCarthy nieces and nephews to immigrate to Massachusetts. Thus she extended into another generation the helping hand she had received from older McCarthy relatives who had come to Haverhill in the 19th century (see p. 14).

FRANCIS CRONIN. Frank Cronin was born in Cork City, Co. Cork, in 1886. He came to Haverhill and lived at Mrs. Ray's boardinghouse on Essex Street while he worked for the Campbell Coal Company. He served as a private in the infantry in WW I. After the war he married Mary Kiley. They bought a home at 182 Franklin Street where they raised their family. Frank continued to work as a truck driver. He died in 1952.

MARY KILEY CRONIN. Mary Kiley was born in Mitchellstown, Co. Cork, in 1895. She lived in Lawrence, Massachusetts, after immigrating and worked as a housekeeper for a local doctor. She and Frank Cronin had five children. Daniel became a priest, Mary married Bartlett Maddix and lives in Michigan, Lillian married Ernest Lupi of Haverhill, Francis married Celeste Dufresne and died in Haverhill in 1988, and Eileen, the youngest, married Vincent Breglia and lives in Methuen. The mix of nationalities among the Cronin in-laws says much about the Americanization of the Irish.

THE GLISPIN/SHUGHRUE FAMILY. Michael Shughrue (1854–1927) emigrated in 1880 from Killarney, Co. Kerry. He operated a grocery store on So. Elm Street. He married Mary Crowley Breen (1856–1935), a widow, in 1891. Her daughter Julia was raised by Shughrue along with their own children. Julia married Joseph Glispin, whose family had come from Kilkenny. His mother, Margaret Hogan Glispin, lived with Julia and Joe. This photo was taken about 1913. Pictured are (front) Irene Collins, an orphan adopted by the Shughrues, Francis Glispin (1911–19), Julia Glispin (1881–1959) holding baby Mary (1913–79), John Glispin (1909–78), and an unidentified girl from a Boston orphan train; (rear) Joseph Glispin (1877–1960), Mary (Mrs. Michael Jr.) Shughrue (1882–1963), Margaret Shughrue, Michael Shughrue Jr. (1883–1933), and Margaret Hogan Glispin (1844–1930).

O'SHEA/LEARY MARRIAGE. John and Catherine (McCarthy) O'Shea, both from Co. Cork, provided the groom. John and Catherine (McMullen) Leary, American-born of Irish parents, provided the bride. The occasion was the wedding of T. Joseph O'Shea to Esther Leary at Sacred Hearts Church, Bradford, in June 1936. Joe O'Shea started to work for the Hamel Leather Company when he was 14. He rose to the ranks of vice president. He and Esther had three children: John, Maureen, and Patricia. Their family home was on South Summer Street, Bradford.

McAleer Family, 1920. Francis McAleer was born in Co. Tyrone in 1869. His family moved to France when he was a child, and it was from there he immigrated to America in 1883. Nora Lucey, born in 1874 in Banteeer, Co. Cork, immigrated in 1893 to join her three sisters in Haverhill. Francis and Nora married in 1900. He was a life insurance agent. They set up home on Bellevue Avenue in what was at that time an enclave of Irish immigrants. They later moved to 5th and then 6th Avenue. Here they pose in 1920 with all eight of their children. In front are Harold, Francis, Roseanne, Nora, and Edward. In rear are Mary Alice, Evelina, John Francis, Joseph, and Ernest.

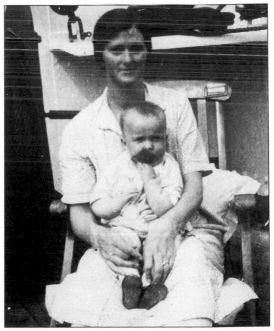

Mary Lysaght Hoar on a Visit to Ireland. Mary Lysaght (see p. 65) married Patrick Hoar (see p. 79) in 1918. In 1928 she made a visit to her home in Ireland and took with her two of her children. She is shown here with her baby daughter Patricia on the deck of the steamship *Thuringia* while on the return voyage to America.

JOHN BRESNAHAN AND SEVEN SONS. John Bresnahan of Tralee, Co. Kerry, began a moving and storage business in Haverhill near his home at 8 Dexter Street. He and his wife Margaret Ryan had three daughters and seven sons. John poses with his sons about the early 1930s. In front are C. Edward (1907–1976), Paul (1914–1976), John Sr. (1862–1948), and Joseph (1909–1983). In rear are Dan (1899–?), Jim, known as Duke (1905–1944), Bill (1912–?), and John (1901–52).

NORA BRODERICK AMBROSE AND EIGHT CHILDREN. In front are Agnes, Kathleen, Nora, Mary, and Helen. In rear are Charlie, Henry, Benjamin, and John ("Spike"). The occasion was the 50th anniversary of Nora's wedding to Benjamin Ambrose. Benjamin had died in 1916 when most of his offspring were still children. The Ambrose family home was at 24 Dexter Street. John "Spike" Ambrose became a Haverhill police officer (see p. 128).

THE RYAN MEN. James "Scagey" Ryan poses with his seven sons. The occasion was the wedding of his son Luke about 1942. In front are Fr. Jim (see p. 121), "Scagey," Luke, and Dan. In rear are John, Anthony (see p. 79), Mike (see p. 116), and Paul, who played semi-pro football and was coach of the Haverhill High football teams of the 1950s. In addition to the seven sons, James and Ellen Ryan had daughters Helen and Mary (see p. 35), and Anna and Bernadette (see below).

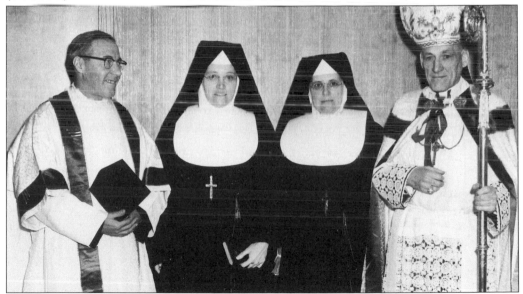

THREE RYANS AND A CARDINAL. The goal of many Irish families was to have a child enter the religious life. James and Ellen Ryan had the good fortune to have three children do so. Pictured from left to right are Fr. James and his twin sister, Anna (Sr. Mariana), and their sister Bernadette (Sr. Prudentia). Both nuns were members of the Sisters of Saint Joseph, who staffed St. James and Sacred Hearts Schools. On the right is the familiar craggy face of Boston's beloved Cardinal Archbishop, Richard J. Cushing.

THREE DRISCOLL SISTERS. Honora (Hanna) Donovan and Patrick Driscoll had emigrated from Ballydehob, Co. Cork, in the mid-1860s. They brought with them their infant son, Cornelius (see p. 30). Eight more children were born to them in America. The Driscolls ran a boardinghouse and saloon/billiards parlor on Essex Street. One daughter died in infancy, a second, Mary Carrigg, died as a young wife. Ellen (Nelly), left, was born in 1877. She married Charles Ford in 1898 and eventually moved to New Jersey. Agnes, center, was born in 1886 and married Harry Kershaw in 1904. They had four children. Agnes died in 1967. Julia, right, was born in 1872, and she married Charles Sheridan and had two sons. Julia died in 1955.

LEO DRISCOLL. Wilfred Leo was the youngest of Pat and Hanna Driscoll's nine children. He was only 18 months old when his father was burned to death in a house fire. Ten years later his mother died. His sister Julia and his oldest brother, Connie, helped to raise him. For many years, Leo worked for his brother-in-law John Carrigg's Star Laundry. Later, with the end of prohibition, he opened Driscoll & Kelly's Tavern on Main Street. Leo married Alice Bryant in 1933. After she died, he lived with his nephew Harold Carrigg, Haverhill's city treasurer. Leo died in 1973.

THE DANIEL LEAHY FAMILY. Dan (see p. 4) and Nora (Murphy) Leahy were married in 1910 in Haverhill. They had eight children. Here they all pose during an outing to Salisbury Beach. It must have been a special occasion for they are all dressed up. Perhaps the day was August 15, the Feast of the Assumption, a day that Irish people traditionally went to the ocean to walk in the water and pray to the Blessed Virgin. In front are Anne, Martin, Daniel, David, and Catherine. In rear are Dan, Nora, Rita, Margaret, and Elizabeth.

"NEILUS" AND MINNIE DONOVAN. Cornelius Donovan was born in Ballydehob, Co. Cork, in 1869. He immigrated to Haverhill in 1892. His aunt, Hanna Donovan Driscoll (see p. 108), had been the first of many in the family—and from that part of Ireland—to come to the city. His wife, Mary (Minnie) Hosford, had been born in Co. Armagh. They married in 1901 and had two children: Cornelius Joseph and Mary Kathleen. Neilus worked for the railroad and their home was on So. New Street, near the Bradford Depot. Here, he keeps a tight grip on his pipe while posing for the photographer.

BILL AND MARY BOLAND AND FRIENDS. William P. Boland was born in Lowell of Irish parents. He moved to Haverhill when he was 15 to live with his older brother, Tom, a sign painter. Tom was the husband of Mary Cronin (see p. 9). Bill Boland began a painting and paperhanging business and met Mary Linnehan, who was teaching at the Rocks Village School. They are shown here with some friends in the early 1920s, shortly before their marriage in 1925. Pictured from left to right are (front) Lillian Cummings, Mary Linnehan, Berenice (Bunny) Marcotte (who married Frank Cronin), and unidentified; (rear) Frank Cummings, Bill Boland, and Frank and Andrew Cronin (see below).

JAMES AND MARY CRONIN 50TH ANNIVERSARY. Twenty-five years after the picture on page 9 was taken, the Cronin family assembled again. This time in 1934 it was to celebrate the Golden Wedding Anniversary of James and Mary. Everyone posed as they had in 1909. In front are Nellie Cronin Higgins, and James, Mary, and Andrew Cronin. Seated on arms of couch are Dr. Edward and William Cronin. In rear are Mary Cronin Boland and James, John, Frank, and Julia Cronin.

110

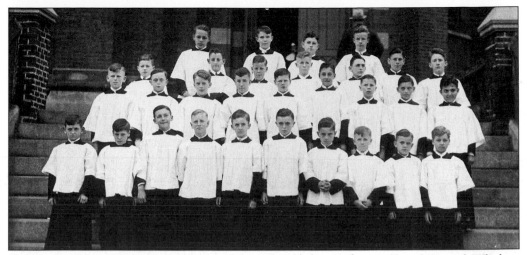

ST. JAMES BOYS CHOIR, 1935. Pictured here from left to right are (front) Daniel Whalen, Robert Kelly, Robert Powers, Raymond Roy, Gerald Shannon, Laurence Hanover, Robert LaBranch, Vincent Driscoll, John Cronin, and Paul Cote; (second row) Richard Dorr, William Powers, Edward Canarie, Donald Lucier, Daniel Cronin (see p. 103), Henry Miller, Robert Shaw, Joseph Hurley, and Norman Beaudry; (third row) William Riley, David Armitage, John Lane, William Flanagan, Paul Sweeney, Paul Lalumiere, and James Canarie; (fourth row) Aloysius Murphy, Leader John Dorr, James Somers, and Martin Wrenn.

REV. MICHAEL HOULIHAN. Fr. Houlihan, right, was the son of John Houlihan (1853–1935) and Annie Sheehan (1853–1936). Both emigrated from Rathmore, Co. Kerry, Annie in 1873 and John in 1882. The couple was married in 1886 and their only child, Michael, was born the next year. Michael graduated from St. James High School and attended both Holy Cross and Boston College before being ordained a priest in 1915. A recently published memoir by a Kerry relative notes the many times that the family returned to visit, including a trip the year of Michael's ordination. For many years, Fr. Houlihan served as state chaplain to the Hibernians. At his funeral in 1973, the Irish Ambassador and the Irish Consul in Boston were present to recognize his services to Ireland. This picture was taken sometime in the 1930s. The man on the left is Daniel Murphy.

JUDGE JOHN J. RYAN SR. John J. Ryan was the son of Michael and Honora (Burke). Michael (1831–1903) immigrated in 1852. Honora (1833–1906) immigrated in 1851. The couple was married in 1852. In 1870, they were living near St. Gregory's Church, and Michael worked in a hat factory. They had four children. Bridget Burke, Honora's sister, was also living with them. John J. Ryan was born in 1871, graduated from Haverhill High School, Holy Cross College, and Boston University School of Law. He began a law practice in 1900, and in 1906, the year his mother died, he was appointed a justice of the Central District Court. Ryan married Elizabeth O'Brien (see p. 45), and they had three children. Judge Ryan died suddenly in 1935. He was 64.

JUDGE DANIEL CAVAN. Cavan's parents were Jeremiah, born in Ireland in 1853, immigrated in 1874, and Mary Sullivan. She was born in Ireland in 1854 and immigrated in 1867. Daniel was born in 1885, graduated from St. James High School and St. Charles College. He earned his law degree from Boston University and began practice in Haverhill in 1909. His sister Margaret was also a law school graduate, and for many years she was the only female attorney in Haverhill. Daniel Cavan was appointed a special justice for the Northern Essex Central District Court in 1913 and presiding justice in 1934. In 1916 he married Margaret Ring who had taught in local schools for ten years after graduating from Lowell Normal School. She died after a brief illness in 1935. Judge Cavan died at 69 in 1954.

MICHAEL H. MCCARTHY, LIQUOR DEALER. Michael was born in Arlington, Massachusetts, in 1854 to immigrant parents Michael and Hannah McCarthy. The family moved to Lawrence in 1863, and Michael began working in the textile mills. When his father died, Michael, 16, moved to Haverhill and had his own business within two years. For many years, McCarthy ran a liquor business on Essex Street. With prohibition, he shifted over to wholesale drugs and groceries. He was in business until he died in 1937 at the age of 83. McCarthy married Catherine Maney in 1877. They were the first couple to be married at a nuptial Mass rather than the traditional brief service in the rectory. The McCarthys celebrated their golden anniversary in 1927 at their summer home in Boar's Head, Hampton Beach, New Hampshire. They had seven children: Charles, Joseph, John, Wilfred, Pauline, Mary Alice, and Celia.

JOE HERLIHY AND HIS ORCHESTRA. "The Pride of New England" was the label attached to Joe Herlihy's orchestra when it appeared at the Roseland Ballroom in New York City. Joe, center of the rear row, and his brother Walter, fourth left in the front row, were the sons of John Herlihy from Co. Kerry and Mary Ann Maroney, Co. Clare. For over ten years their orchestra played in all the leading ballrooms throughout the East Coast. They discovered a number of performers who would go on to achieve national fame, including singer Rudy Vallee, comedian Jerry Colonna, and "Banjo King" Eddie Peabody. The brothers eventually went to work for the family business.

THOMAS LAHEY (1854–1938). Thomas Lahey is best known to history as the father of Dr. Frank Lahey, world-renowned surgeon and founder of the Lahey clinic. However, Thomas had already earned acclaim while his son was still a young man. Thomas was born in Stoneham. His father, born in Ireland, had moved to Newfoundland as a young man, and it was there that Thomas's siblings were born. Lahey moved to Haverhill, married Honora Power, and established the contracting and bridge-building business for which he was well known. His specialty was granite work, and he had quarries throughout New Hampshire and granite works, not only in Haverhill, but in Lawrence and Chelmsford, too. Thomas died in 1938 at the age of 84.

HONORA POWER LAHEY (1854–1921). Honora was born in England where her Irish parents, Nicholas and Margaret, lived for a few years before moving to Haverhill in 1857. Her father would become a leading undertaker with rooms located opposite St. James Church on Primrose Street. Honora married Thomas Lahey in the late 1870s. They had two sons, Frank and Thomas Dayton. Dayton died in 1885 when he was two years old, and Frank was raised as an only child. Nora Power Lahey died in 1921. She was 67 but had lived to see her son established as one of the nation's most acclaimed surgeons.

FRANK LAHEY AND HHS TRACK TEAM. Frank Howard Lahey was born in 1880 to Thomas and Honora. He attended Haverhill High School and, though never large in stature, played football, baseball, and ran track. He is shown in this photo on the right of the third row. His teammate, Joe Lee, seated front row left, was arguably Haverhill High School's greatest all-around athlete and remained close to Frank Lahey all his life. Lahey graduated from Harvard Medical School and began his specialty in surgery. The Lahey Clinic he founded is considered one of America's great medical centers.

HAVERHILL DOCTORS ON HALE HOSPITAL STAFF. This 1925 photograph of the medical staff at Haverhill's Hale Hospital shows many doctors of Irish heritage. Pictured here are (front) Frank Coffin, Hugh Donahue (see p. 44), Chas. Durant, John Sproull, Adelbert Hubbell, John Bryant, and J. Joseph Fitzgerald; (middle) Hyman Mysel, Henry Armitage, Timothy Cotter, George Connor, Wm. Ferrin, Henry Kapp, John L. O'Toole, and Guy Richardson; (back) J. Edward Kelleher (see p. 62), Eugene Gale, Elmer Bagnall, Raymond Root, Lucien Chaput, Thomas Stone, Wm. Porell, and John J. Kearney.

BISHOP DESMOND AND CLASSMATES. Daniel Desmond (see p. 31) was born in Haverhill in 1884. His father, Daniel, was a cobbler from Bandon, Co. Cork. His mother, Katherine Lynch, was a native of Andover, Massachusetts. Dan graduated from St. James High in 1900, entered the seminary after completing Holy Cross College, and was ordained in 1911. He served as a chaplain in WW I. Soon after his return from service, Fr. Desmond was appointed director of Catholic Charities in Somerville, and, though he had yet to become a pastor, he was elevated to the position of Bishop of Alexandria, Louisiana, in 1932. He is pictured here at a reunion with his high school classmates. They are shown in what was called the "gun room" of the pastor of St. James, Fr. Lyons. The man in the rear is John Callahan, a pharmacist. Seated far right are Mamie Sullivan Legault and Martha Devlin Dorsey, wife of Michael Dorsey Jr. Other women in the class were Malena Carberry, Nora Cavan, Katherine Couney, Mary Dugas, Grace and Regina Gage, Helen Powers, and Gertrude Ramsay. Classmate Mary Wallace became Sister Ita and could not be present.

SJHS FOOTBALL TEAM, 1929. One of many great football teams that performed for St. James High in the 1920s and 1930s was the 1929 team. The school body was still predominantly Irish in heritage, which is reflected in the names of the players. From left to right are (front) Arthur Mullen, Sid Lafey (see p. 98), Francis Smith, Bill Fenlon, Eddie Theriault, and Joe Farley; (rear) Leonard McCaughey, John Horgan, Joe Bescher, Ed Buckley, Mike Ryan (see p. 107) and his cousin Jack Dorsey (see p. 104), and Coach Edward "Bodger" Carroll (see p. 31).

FLAHERTY FAMILY IN IRELAND. Morgan (1860–1941) and Hannah (1870–1952) O'Flaherty emigrated from Co. Galway soon after Irish Independence. Some of the family appears in the Haverhill City Directory for the first time in 1922 when they were living at 4 1/2 Dexter Street. Two years later they were in their home at 3 Seventh Avenue. This photo was taken outside their home in Ireland about 1910–12. Maurice (1900–1983) is the young lad playing the button accordion, seated right. His parents are seated center with Bernard standing between them. The other seated man is oldest son Morgan Jr. (1889–1968), and to his right, with the toy horse, is Anthony (1908–1957). Only Timothy, not shown, stayed in Ireland. The others in the family who moved to Haverhill were Agnes (Mahoney), Celia (1914–1991), Ida, Eileen, Kate, Mary, and Joe. One daughter died young in Ireland.

"Danno" O'Mahoney Poster.

"Danno" O'Mahoney, from Dreenlamane, Ballydehob, Co. Cork, received world-wide recognition when he became the world wrestling champion in the 1930s. This was a time when wrestling was a serious business, and the good-looking, powerfully built Irishman had an enormous following. None could have been more partisan than his admirers in Haverhill, for there were hundreds of immigrants, and children of immigrants, who came from his section of Co. Cork. He had come out of a tradition of amateur field and track events, such as leaping and jumping contests, weight-throwing, and long-distance running, and his father before him had been known for his athleticism. So, the appearance of "Danno" at the St. James fund-raiser in 1935 was a surefire money maker.

"Danno" with Cousins.

O'Mahoney's nearest neighbors in Dreenlamane were his cousins, the O'Donovans, children of John and Ellen (O'Mahoney). Five of that family had come to Haverhill (see p. 109) along with dozens of aunts, uncles, and cousins. Those that stayed at home continue to have family members living in the old homestead, and their nearest neighbor is "Danno's" elderly brother. Julia O'Mahoney, Dan's aunt, is seated. Standing are Mary Donovan McSweeney, who lived in Haverhill for a half dozen years before returning home, Danno O'Mahoney, and Timmy Joe, Mary, Ellen, and Patrick O'Donovan, who was all set to emigrate when it became his responsibility to take over the family farm.

Seven

THE TRADITION
CONTINUES

SACRED HEARTS PARISH HONOREES. In 1956, Sacred Hearts parish honored a group of men whose service to the parish dated back to the early years of the century. Many of them were Irish immigrants, or children of immigrants. Pictured from left to right are (front row) William Lavin, Joseph Hanlon, Rt. Rev. Michael F. Madden (pastor and Bradford native), John McKeigue, and Timothy Donovan; (second row) William Doucette, Charles Cassily, Eugene Breault, Dennis Murphy, Michael Coughlin, Timothy McKeigue, and John Cronin (see p.9); (back row) Jeremiah Donovan and Jeremiah McCarthy.

THE O'BRIENS FROM DUNBEACON. Margaret, Ellen, and John O'Brien emigrated from Dunbeacon, Co. Cork, in the 1890s. They are seen here at a family wedding many decades later surrounded by two generations of their families. From left to right are (front) Marie Burchell Kelly, Mrs. Jack (Mary) Burchell, Celia Burchell, Margaret O'Brien Purcell, John O'Brien, Ellen O'Brien Burchell, Ed Hogg, Christine O'Brien Hogg, Mrs. Joe (Helen) O'Brien, and Anna O'Brien O'Connor; (rear) Mrs. Paul (Theresa) O'Brien, Audrey Burchell, Bill Burchell, Margaret Purcell Lucey, Joe O'Brien, Anne Burchell Moynihan, Ambrose Purcell, Mrs. Ambrose (Helen) Purcell, Paul O'Brien, Bernard Purcell, and Jack Moynihan (son of Anne Burchell Moynihan).

JAMES P. CLEARY, LAWYER. James Cleary was born in Boston in 1890, and, after receiving his law degree from Boston University and serving in WW I, he moved to Haverhill to join Judge John J. Ryan in practice. He also practiced with John Ryan Jr. and his own son, James Jr. In 1921, he married Ryan's cousin Dorothy Lennon, daughter of John and Mary (Ryan) Lennon (see p. 78). Cleary had been one of the organizers of the national American Legion in 1919. He served on Draft Board Seven for ten years. He was also president of the Haverhill Chamber of Commerce. Cleary is shown here about to introduce former Governor Maurice Tobin, who went on to serve in President Harry Truman's Cabinet. Cleary died in 1958 at the age of 67.

FLORRY AND ANNIE SULLIVAN. Florence Patrick Sullivan was born in Ballydehob, Co. Cork, about 1888. He immigrated to America in 1912, staying first in Lynn where he had brothers. He then moved to Haverhill, a place where he had numerous Sullivan, Mahoney, and Donovan cousins. His brother Jerry found him a job as a switchman on the railroad. He married Annie Fitzgerald (see p. 76) in 1921. This photo was taken when they celebrated their 25th wedding anniversary in 1946. Florry died in 1954 and Annie in 1977.

HAVERHILL NATIVE-BORN PRIESTS. A new Catholic church was dedicated in Haverhill in 1956. It was named St. John the Baptist, and its first pastor was Haverhill-native Rev. James P. Ryan. It was an appropriate occasion to gather many locally born priests and a reminder of the strong ties between heritage and religion for many of Irish ancestry. From left to right are (front) Rt. Rev. John J. Lynch, Fr. Ryan, Bishop Jeremiah F. Minihan, Rt. Rev. Michael F. Madden, and Rev. James H. O'Connell; (back) Rev. Harvey J. Fortier, Rev. Thomas J. Lafey, Rev. Gerald D. Desmond (a nephew of Bishop Desmond, p. 116), Rev. Daniel J. Mahoney (a nephew of Anna Mahoney Dwyer, p. 127), Rev. Alfred C. Delva, OMI, Rev. Joseph V. Mullen, Rev. William L. Keville, Rev. Gerald B. Horgan (see p. 17), and Rev. John J. McCarthy.

THE HOURIHAN SISTERS. Bridget (Bridey) and Margaret (Gretta) Hourihan came from Drinagh, Co. Cork, after WW II. They were part of a fourth wave of Irish immigrants and were coming to a city where there were three generations of relatives. Both went to work as waitresses at Bradford Junior College. Bridey, seated, became the housekeeper for President Dorothy Bell in the president's residence on campus in 1957. The President's House is the building behind them. Gretta, standing, became the assistant director of the Food Service.

PATRICK "PACKY" LINEHAN. Packy Linehan was the son of Limerick immigrants John and Bridget. Born in 1895, he began playing the violin while still a very young boy. He became one of Greater Haverhill's premier fiddlers, in great demand at everything from large balls at Hibernian Hall to intimate kitchen "rackets," the informal parties where music and dance were inevitable. He married Mary Cash in the 1920s. Their son Patrick Jr. (see p. 98) was killed during WW II. Mary died in 1964, Packy in 1983.

DR. DAN AND RAY TAFFE. Daniel Raymond ("Ray") Taffe, born in 1899, was the son of Daniel Taffe and Brigid Lucey. Brigid was the sister of Nora McAleer (see p. 105). Ray's father was killed by a trolley car in 1916, the year Ray graduated from St. James High School, yet the young man was able to attend Boston College for three years and serve in WW 1. He married Ethel Robitaille in 1923 and they had three children: Elaine, Dr. Daniel R., and Theresa (Mrs. John) Connolly. Technically, Ray worked for the post office, but in reality he worked for all the people of Haverhill, including those with Irish blood: Hibernians, Foresters, March of Dimes, Council on Aging, Citizen Center, St. James parish—he gave thousands of hours of his time. Ray, on the right, and his son, Dr. Dan, on the left, are shown here entertaining at a Hale Hospital benefit. Ray Taffe died in December 1988 just short of his 90th birthday.

ANCIENT ORDER OF HIBERNIANS. For over 100 years, the Hibernians had been the premier Irish organization in Haverhill. At its height, there were two divisions for men and an auxiliary for women. Membership peaked at over 600 in the late 1920s. Between 1913 and 1947 they had their own building at 81 Winter Street, and this was the scene not only of meetings but of dances, pool and bowling tournaments, theatrical performances, and parties. The women's auxiliary had a revival in the post-war years, but, eventually, it, too, was dissolved as its brother divisions had already done. This picture dates from the mid-1960s. In front are D. Raymond Taffe (president of the men's division), Bishop Jerry Minihan, Rev. John Finn of St. James Parish, and Alice (Mrs. Paul) Chase. In rear are Rose Moynihan Batchelder (president of the women's division), Geraldine Rheaume, four state and county officials, and Mayor Paul I. Chase.

CITY CLERK BERNARD DONAHUE.

Bernard Donahue's lineage was solidly Irish. His parents were Bernard and Kate (Carroll) Donahue (see p. 42). His Donahue and Carroll grandparents were among the Irish pioneers to Haverhill. Bernard was born in 1903. After graduating from Haverhill High School, he went to Georgetown University and a graduate year at its Foreign Service School. He was back in Haverhill by 1932 and went into the retail liquor business. In 1938, he was appointed city clerk, a position he held for the next 20 years. He is shown in this photograph in the city clerk's office in city hall. For a while, in 1949, he was acting mayor following the resignation for ill health of Mayor Albert Glynn. Donahue retired in 1958 after experiencing a series of cerebral spasms and died three years later at the age of 58.

RAY MCNAMARA AND ALBERT GLYNN. Few people were better known in Haverhill in the 1940s than Irish-Americans Raymond McNamara and Albert Glynn. Ray, a staunch Democrat, had been appointed postmaster in 1939, a post previously held by his brother George and his father Lott. He was a most public-spirited citizen, who was regularly called upon to head up fund-raising drives and civic organizations. Albert Glynn, son of a barber, had become a shoe manufacturer and was as staunch a Republican as McNamara was a Democrat. He was elected mayor of Haverhill in 1938 as a fiscal conservative, bucking a nation-wide Democratic dominance. He served until 1949 when he resigned because of ill health. In this photo, Postmaster McNamara presents Mayor Glynn with a sheet of the first Air Mail stamps issued by the post office.

1941

1946

PHILIP H. STACY
Alderman, 1941-1946

THOMAS F. MONAHAN
Alderman, 1941-1946

WILLIAM J. O'LEARY
Alderman, 1944-1946

HON. ALBERT W. GLYNN
Mayor, 1941-1946

EARLE V. TAILLON
Alderman, 1946

CITY GOVERNMENT, 1942–46. Any discussion of Haverhill's Irish heritage must take note of a particular difference between this city and most other industrial cities in Massachusetts where there were a significant number of Irish immigrants. Haverhill was the marked exception where the local government did not come under the control of Irish bosses, usually of the Democratic persuasion. Though people of Irish background were regularly elected to office, no one of that heritage became mayor until Albert Glynn was elected in 1938, and he ran as a Republican! However, by WW II, Irish names had become predominant in local government. This portfolio represents the mayor and aldermen who served while WW II was in process. Four of them, in addition to Albert Glynn, had Irish forebears. Thomas Monahan, son of Thomas and Margaret (Fitzgerald) Monahan, is shown at upper right. At center left is William J. O'Leary, son of Cornelius and Elizabeth (Fitzgerald) O'Leary. At lower left is Atty. Daniel J. Minihan, son of Timothy and Nora (Duggan) Minihan (see p. 75), and in the center is James M. Costello, son of John and Katherine (Marrin) Costello. Costello was first elected an alderman in 1928.

MICHAEL O'DEA AND THE CRYSTAL LAKE BOTTLING PLANT. Michael O'Dea came from the vicinity of Galway City, Co. Galway. He had taken part in Ireland's war for independence from the British and spent time in an English jail for his activities. He immigrated to America about 1926 and was living in Lynn. One afternoon, after a particularly successful trip to Rockingham Race Track, he was returning home by way of Route 97 (Broadway) in Haverhill. On the spur of the moment he decided to invest his winnings in a bottling company that would take advantage of the pure water in Crystal Lake. His partner was Arthur Lecolst. The bottling plant produced a full line of flavored soft drinks, including Moxie, that strong-flavored drink that is a reminder of why sodas were known in New England as "tonics." The soft drinks were sold under the name Old Kerry. Why was a Galway man using a Kerry name? He never said. Michael O'Dea is in the white jacket. Donald McKay, an employee, is in the rear.

FRANK O'DEA, JOHN NOLAN, ET AL. AT OLD KERRY. Michael "Frank" O'Dea and his first cousin, John Nolan, emigrated from Clarinbridge, Galway City, after WW II and worked with Frank's uncle at his Crystal Lake Bottling Company. They are shown here about 1950. Shown from left are Frank O'Dea, unidentified, John Nolan, and John Lecolst, whose uncle was a co-owner. John Nolan became a Haverhill police officer. Frank O'Dea continued to work for the bottling company until it closed in the recent past.

ANN C. BOLAND AND ANNA MAHONEY DWYER. Anna Mahoney was born in Rock Chapel, Co. Cork, in 1887. She came to Haverhill with the help of her aunt, Julia Mahoney Fitzgerald, and husband Maurice (see p. 22). Anna worked as a domestic for Louis B. Mayer when that future movie mogul was in Haverhill. She was a supervisor for the Wason Shoe Company until the owner died. Then Anna, her husband Eddie Dwyer, and Eddie Curtin (brother of Daniel) started the Victory Wood Heel Company. Eddie died in 1939. Following the war, Anna was asked by Fr. Timothy Donovan, pastor of St. James, to take over the Catholic Charities Bureau in Haverhill. Anna, right, is shown about 1940 with her young cousin, Ann Catherine Boland, the daughter of Bill and Mary Boland (see p. 110). Anna died in 1968.

MICHAEL FITZGERALD FAMILY. Michael, from Tralee, and Bridget (Moynihan) from Rathmore, both in Co. Kerry, were married in 1899. According to the 1910 Federal Census, Michael was 38, had immigrated in 1889, was a naturalized citizen, and employed as a city laborer. Bridget was 34, had immigrated in 1885, and had borne five children, four of whom were alive. This photo was probably taken in the early to mid-1940s. From left to right are (front) William Fitzgerald, Esther (Mrs. Emilio) Tondi, Geraldine (Mrs. Edmund) Burke, and Michael and Bridget Fitzgerald; (standing) James Fitzgerald, Julia (Mrs. Haig) Babolian, Jeremiah "Judgy" Fitzgerald, and Anna (Mrs. Theodore) Pelosi. Michael died in 1948. Bridget outlived her son William, who died in 1960. She died at 94 in 1971 soon after her grandson, Ted Pelosi, began his long career in city government.

HAVERHILL POLICE DEPARTMENT, 1942. The names say it all about the presence of the Irish in the mid-20th century. Pictured from left to right are (front) Deputy William Gavin, Chief Henry J. Lynch, and Capt. Thomas Madden; (second row) Sgt. William Collins, Sgt. George Hefferan, Capt. Joseph U. Ryan, Insp. Calvin Long, Sgt. Charles Dillon, Lt. Insp. Ovila Lagasse, Charles Cassily, and Ralph Woodburn; (third row) Timothy Mahoney, John J. Wholley (1), Natale Parodi, William Foren, Ralph Clough, Laburton Goodwin, Hiram Eldridge, and John F. Coughlin; (fourth row) James Cronin, Daniel Healy, Victor Champagne, Daniel ("Neil") Coughlin, John J. McGovern, John ("Spike") Ambrose, James Reaney, James Snee, and Harry Hunter; (fifth row) William Lane, Frank Burnham, C. Edward Driscoll, Joseph Cox, Patrick Somers, Joseph Mangarpan, Thomas Trainor, John Leary, and Philip McDonald; (sixth row) Martin Sullivan, Herman Fauth, E. Hollis Bruce, John McGowan, George Bruce, J. Henry Woelflein, John J. Regan, Thomas Davidson, and John J. Wholley (2); (seventh row) Harold Fitzgerald, Guy Littlefield, Joseph Decoteau, Andrew Sheehan, Melvin Batchelder, Mark Ricker, Floyd Wheeler, William Barrett, and John J. Butler.